MANAGEMENT OF BUSINESS ETHICS

MANAGEMENT OF BUSINESS ETHICS

Sidney C. Sufrin

National University Publications
KENNIKAT PRESS // 1980
Port Washington, N. Y. // London

Manufactured in the United States of America

Published by
Kennikat Press Corp.
Port Washington, N.Y. / London

Library of Congress Cataloging in Publication Data

Sufrin, Sidney C   1910–
  Management of business ethics.

  (National university publications)
  Bibliography: p.
  Includes index.
  1. Business ethics. 2. Management. I. Title.
HF5387.S83   174'.4   79-433
ISBN 0-8046-9243-2

For my extensive—
and somewhat extended—
family

CONTENTS

PREFACE

This is a book about business ethics, which is not unrelated to ethics more generally viewed.

At the onset the reader should be aware that the work is not a manual of licit behavior, a cook-book of how to prepare a just, moral, ethical bill of fare which satisfies the consumer and assures success and praise for the producer. It is not that ambitious; nor, the argument of the work insists, is such a menu of business (social or private, for that matter) behavior possible.

What we attempt in this little book is to talk about the concepts of ethics and morality, and try to expose how social actions may be morally viewed.

In doing this, we use, as one must in a discussion at once so difficult and so ordinary, words which are in common usage. But the common use of words often carries with it different meanings and shades of meanings in different contexts. Possibly this is what makes ethical discussions easy to engage in. The difficulty is coming up with acceptable, systematic generalizations. All one can expect from the reader is his or her willingness to accept, for the time being, the definitions which are used.

My purpose in writing this book is to devise and develop some notions of how right and wrong for business are, or should be, determined, so that the ideas can be used in understanding the most significant of all social phenomena—Social Change, in which business plays such a large role.

It seems to me that to talk about social change without some moral aspects is to miss the whole point of civilization and the civilizing process which is somehow based on Truth, Goodness, and Beauty.

The reader should bear in mind that moral and ethical concerns do not generally fill the minds of active people. Business requires active people, not monastic or philosophic persons leading lives of ethical contemplation. Ethical ideas are perhaps mainly reflected on in business after an action is completed, or vaguely in prospect as an exercise in legitimation. Nevertheless ethical considerations are implicit in most, perhaps all, social actions.

I am in the debt of many colleagues. My old friends Professors Abraham Veinus of Syracuse University and George Odiorne, my colleague at Amherst, each suggested I write down some of the ideas we had talked about. In a general way, this book is the result. Professors Joseph Finnerty, Thomas Schneeweis, Anthony Butterfield, Van Court Hare, Arthur Elkins, Robert McGarrah, Vere Chappell and Leone Stein were properly critical and patient. To them I owe my thanks, even if we did not always convince each other.

Mrs. Vesta Powers and her staff obligingly read my handwriting and produced a transcript. Again my thanks.

Mr. John Parke went beyond what an editor is normally expected to do. Ms. Debbie Bickford helped in putting the typescript together. I am indebted to both.

But my major gratitude is due my wife, Irene, who, morning after morning listened to brief essays, delivered across the breakfast table. She never once told me I was talking nonsense which sometimes I was. My debt to her is great indeed.

MANAGEMENT OF BUSINESS ETHICS

ABOUT THE AUTHOR

Sidney C. Sufrin is a Professor of Business Economics at the University of Massachusetts School of Business in Amherst, Massachusetts. He has maintained contacts with business and government throughout his academic career. He is the author of numerous articles in various technical and philosophical journals as well as several books on economics and business.

1

A STRUCTURE OF BUSINESS ETHICS

Looking back over history, and looking around the world, we are impressed by the achievement of society. By "society" we mean the system which is a complex of science, technology, and ideologies making up the United States and western Europe. What will happen when, as, and if Japan is joined by other nations of the Orient, when, as, and if the Soviet Union and its train of nations and Africa and the Arab states each adopt or grow into the Western, American world of science and technology, and adjust their ideologies, is an open question.

But the quantified life—that is the life judged by the number of automobiles and television sets, by the average life expectancy, and by all the other numbers of the *Statistical Abstract*—is only half a life. The qualitative life, the life which pays homage to ideas of goodness, truth, and beauty, is implicit in not only the philosopher's "good life" but in any meaningful life. The scientist, the manager, the factory worker, the foreman—all people who are productive—judge their efforts and endeavors by criteria other than "How much" or "How many."

Social effort and accomplishment in any society are ultimately judged by what we loosely call public opinion and by the value system of the individual doing the judging. Public opinion is, in its ultimate, a legitimation, a moral evaluation of social effort and accomplishment. Public opinion as a moral force reflects or assumes standards as part of the inner architecture of social events and personal behavior. Standards are not easily standardized, with one set being adequate for all times, places, and situations. Standards as part of public opinion, and hence public opinions, are complex and variable. What is sauce for the goose is not always sauce for the gander; what is morally permissible in the marketplace is not always relevant to a university.

The same complexity applies to the standards an individual uses in judging his own work or the efforts of others. We expect more or less of ourselves and of others under differing circumstances. And we perform differently in different situations. Neither the internal nor the external worlds are staled by custom, but are of infinite variety.

Morals and ethics are both social and personal attitudes and values we shall argue in this book; but moral and ethical values are not neat, strong, sharp definitions which can be put in a manual for all to read and follow.

A social system such as business or politics, as opposed to a natural system like astronomy or molecular physics, usually implies some degree of functionality. There need be no reason why stars follow their courses, except the reason of physical laws. But a social system is purposive. It presumably has a goal, for most of us like to think there is a purpose to social behavior. Dysfunctional social systems fail because the interactions of their various parts do not produce appropriate outputs. Even worse, a system may produce outputs that are hurtful to its operation. In a simple but significant sense, a social system is judged by its output—"the bottom line" in contemporary jargon.

To judge a system by its output is to ascribe values to it. Judgment is required to legitimate (or refuse legitimation to) a social system such as a business, a government, or a whole society. Legitimation, in a broad social sense, is dependent on public opinion. A brief discussion will illustrate the complexity of what is often referred to as the fickleness of public opinion.

The Rockefeller family, on the whole, if we interpret the public mind properly, has the reputation for "doing good." The Rockefeller Foundation is a scientific jewel given to the world by that family. Public service and politics have been enriched by the contributions of the Rockefellers. In part this public acceptance may be the result of an effective public relations effort, but P.R. aside, the public mind tends to accept the good works.

Yet only one or two generations ago the Rockefellers' public face was not so clean. The business excesses of the Standard Oil Company, a Rockefeller enterprise, were considered scandalous in many circles. The great Standard Oil case under the Sherman Anti-Trust Act has been used as an illustration in teaching and in the public press, of how a big corporation may destroy competitors and even threaten the underpinnings of capitalism itself.

On the other hand, the Ford family has never quite, in our opinion, been accepted as a force for social good in the same sense as the Rockefellers. The engineering problems of Ford cars which came to glaring light with the federal government's charges about the Pinto's weakness in a rear end collision, and the tendency for Ford's automatic transmissions to shift gears on their own volition has even more recently undermined the company's public image. The Edsel fiasco did not help, nor did the shenanigans of the Ford uncle and nephew, over the control of the Ford empire at the 1979 annual meeting. The family owns a controlling interest in the Ford Motor Company. But before technical automotive weaknesses came to light, the Ford Motor Company was associated with the Ford family, and neither was considered as a great public benefactor (in contrast to the Rockefellers).

The Ford Foundation, a Ford family gift to the nation as well as a tax avoidance device, is many times the size of the Rockefeller Foundation. Both have made great contributions to learning and probably the quality of life. But the Ford enterprise, again in our opinion, has not captured or shared the aura of the Rockefeller Foundation. Public opinion has reacted differently to similar stimuli. These observations are not based on any scientific, statistical research but do seem to reflect current public thinking.

Public opinion, we believe, is an expression of the general ideological evaluation of people, institutions, and events. By ideological evaluation we mean the weighing and ordering—that is, placing people, institutions, and events in a value hierarchy—by great numbers of people. In this they are aided by the news media and the position taken by opinion makers such as politicians, artists, and the clergy. In short, ideology is the complex of social values and evaluations in action. The setting, the style, the output, the purpose, all the attributes of people, institutions, and events, insofar as they are known, are discussed, evaluated, and categorized.

The evaluation and categorization may persist for only a short time; it may change.

The Astors and Carnegies of the last century are largely forgotten as public figures today. J. P. Morgan lingers on in the public memory, although time has changed his image from that of a robber baron to a very rich art collector. The splendiferous and often scandalous private lives of the robber barons are no longer titillating. Lizzie Borden, who was accused of literally taking her immediate family apart, aided by an axe, is better remembered than John Archbold, a Rockefeller partner, a patron of Syracuse University, and the first man named in the anti-trust indictment. The same phenomenon occurs in politics. The Adams family, for all their brilliance, plus a TV series, has never quite been rewarded by a public image like that of the brilliant Jefferson or the saintly Lincoln.

If a business or government has no choices, it is useless, and worse, to complain that nonattainable goals are not attained. The Man of La Mancha's song about dreaming the impossible dream and beating the unbeatable foe may be good theater, but it does not make much operational sense. One can assert that a business "failed" to achieve an ideal goal which *constraints* prevented it from achieving. The ideal goal may have been a necessary one for the continued operation of the firm. For example, the Department of Justice, not feeling a situation falls into the "failing business doctrine," asserts it will bring a legal action against the merger of two companies, one large and one small. But if, in truth, failure to merge will destroy the small company, the Department of Justice is a *force majeure* that the small company cannot combat. To criticize or judge the firm for such a turn of events is akin to criticizing the operation of a natural law that, by its nature, is indifferent to human values.

Judgments in social and economic matters are most trenchant when they criticize behavior because it was misdirected or inept. Freedom of choice on the part of the actors is then assumed. But more is usually implied. Actions are judged (legitimated) on the basis of whom they affect and to what degree. An economy with a high output and high rate of increase of output is subject to criticism if its unemployment rate is considered higher than some desired level. In the late 1970s when United States production and employment were high, the high level of unemployment and the inflation were quite properly seen as significant social failures. Similarly a full employment economy would not gain approval if its output were not up to some standards implicitly or explicitly stated. This is the American criticism of West Germany and Japan at the end of the seventies.

Economic or business systems are generally judged in the light of fairly obvious and simple criteria such as output, price levels, and employment. When causal interrelations, such as interest rates, supply of money, rate of savings, labor participation rates, or foreign trade, are attempted, the analysis and criticism of behavior become impossibly confusing. For neither the mechanisms of the hypothetical system nor the goals of behavior, social or corporate, are specifically known or generally agreed upon.

Implied in such considerations are at least two factors: (1) To what extent was it necessary that the particular system being examined depart from the "ideal system" posited by theorists, and (2) Were such departures the results of individual or social choices currently or previously made?

The first question implies that some obstruction has either developed or been introduced, and should be removed if the system is to be functional. This view is widely applied by economists to monopolies or labor unions. Such institutions, it is held, obstruct the operations of a free market, which is the ideal. This ideal, to our mind at least, confuses a "natural" mechanism with a conventional, social way of organizing and behaving. The second question goes to the issue of what freedom of choice was available to the manager of the enterprise or in the environment of the enterprise.

Implied in these questions of why a system (e.g., a firm) does not work as it should is the notion that the output of the ideal system is an ideal output. The argument that competition produces more social product than noncompetitive social organizations is an argument in which the ends were decided upon to legitimate the means, rather than flowing from the means.[1] The legitimation of business behavior is often based on ideals which are not implicit in ongoing institutions or in managerial capacity or environmental benevolence.

If the malfunction of an enterprise is related to social or personal tampering or improper choice, who benefits and who suffers are consequences, in terms of both of operations and values, to persons and other social systems. Such questions *always* imply some consideration of morality, justice, and ethics. This is so because a non-idealized, actual system always produces an output that is different in dimension, distribution, and implication from the ideal output of an ideal system. If the nature, distribution, and implication of output did not vary from the idealized output, there would have been no reason to examine the particular system for flaw or dysfunction. Any one of the three attributes of output—dimension (size), distribution (who gets what), and implication (effect on other activities)—if it departs from the conceptual norm is sufficient to cause the particular case to be questioned.[2] Novelty in the particular—that is, difference from the ideal—requires legitimation.

Before one can evaluate an enterprise's achievement of a desired goal, one must have some understanding of the institution. This means having a theory, or at least a conceptualization, of the means-end relations involved. In the language of the day, one needs a "model" of what is being considered. Mathematical models have become a faddish necessity in economic and business analyses. But models are only ideals of how a business or institution works, the ideal being simplified by using only essential features. Mathematics (algebra) is used to simplify the complex, and so often makes the specific enterprise incomprehensible to a reader of the analysis.

Insofar as a model explains a social process, it may provide "normative dignity to practical imperatives." That is to say, what is necessary or usual becomes what is good. The legitimation of an institution may provide a yardstick for measuring justice, personally conceived. For example, piece rates are justified because they adjust earnings to output, hence are good. In truth, we all know that the level of piece rates is the result of capital investment, labor skill, organization, and half a hundred other factors, including the working conventions of the workplace. Similarly wise investments in the stock market may result in capital gains. Such gains are often viewed as a reward for wise investment and so are justified. But we all know that chance, inflation, technology, managerial shakeups and changes, and poor management of competitors are salient forces in generating the capital gain. By making a simple model which legitimates what needs legitimation, the problem is solved, at least conceptually. The normative dignity of institutional behavior is the social norm, deviation from which measures the moral or immoral nature of social actions. Legitimation then assumes that the functions of an institution are known

and the evaluation of the material and immaterial outputs are meas-
urable.[3] So much for the moral aspects of models.

Of all the social disciplines, economics has devised the most exhaus-
tive and operationally successful systemic models or paradigms. Yet
it is estimated that no less than half the adjustments to the macro
model are exogenously caused. The system is constantly adjusting
to forces which have their origin outside it, like gremlins upsetting
rather than resolving the confusions of economic life.[4] Frank Knight
used to assert that in social science persuasion is the best way to
win an argument or prove a point. Sheer logic often is less powerful
than persuasion when the universe of discourse is neither tidy nor
very well defined. Polanyi echoes this belief when he asserts that
science generally assesses an argument by its plausibility, which is
related to intuition.[5]

Legitimation or justification of an aberration from the ideal is
not dissimilar from St. Augustine's discussion of the City of God
and the City of Man. The ideal is God's city; the particular, man's.
The output desired is God's, not man's; hence the task of man is to
conform his city, conventions, and law to God's. But such conformity
cannot be totally realized. This theological view is, not so subtly,
carried into economic analysis by the father of our system, Adam
Smith. For him, and for the classical economists generally, the
ordered, competitive economic system provides the best of all
possible outputs and distribution. For Smith the order of individualism and private property are of man and his city. The state,
as opposed to the city of the marketplace, is needed to provide
some political mechanisms and some services. But, by and large,
the market as a natural agency, the scene at once of man's selfishness and sympathy (empathy), solves most of the problems of
morality, justice, and ethics insofar as production and distribution
are concerned. Smith, like the theist Butler, held that selfishness
and a social concern were both inherent in the nature of man. But
the selfishness of each individual leads to competition, which produces
the largest (ideal) output for consumers! The state is a policeman, a
garbage collector, and maybe a schoolteacher. Man's city is the
market where little entrepreneurs unconsciously produce big things.
Really, for Smith business and social organizations (division of labor)
were the secret of societal success.

Legitimation, then, is found, for the classical economists and many business people, in allowing the competitive free market to function, because, by logic and ideology, such markets are the natural producers of the best bottom line. This conclusion, however, is not supported by empirical research. Nor are some of the assumptions used in the analysis—for example, individualism (self-interest), perfect knowledge, and competition of the many—very satisfactory to its critics. For Smith and many of his present-day disciples, the means are justified by the assumed, ideal ends. Yet the end products of some other socially contrived economic system might be more favorably evaluated by competent observers than the ideal output of the competitive ideal system. Also, the value system which is agreeable to the legitimators of the (competitive) idealized system may not be acceptable either generally, or at different places, to a large part of a society. But we feel a good case can still be made for the market economy on more plausible grounds.

We have used the concepts "moral," "ethical," and "just" without defining them, relying on the common sense, generally accepted, if vague, meanings. These are words whose meanings cannot be tied down because each carries with it overtones of specific values which, while generally and imprecisely agreed upon, are not agreed upon in detail by all members of a society. Particular actions and particular events of a social or economic system inevitably depart from the behavior of ideal, abstract systems.[6] Particulars are what are valued ethically, morally, and from the viewpoint of justice. Particulars, as we suggest, often elicit less universal value agreement than abstract generalities. The definitions we offer are not always those in common use because common usage varies widely in different contexts. There is always an arbitrariness in the conscious artifact of defining a concept. One can only hope that the reader will accept the definitions in the context of the argument being presented. Criticism may, of course, be directed against the argument, but not against the definitions of words and concepts.

Recognizing these limitations, we shall define moral acts by reference to convention as a base. Thus an economic action that conforms to law or convention is morally neutral. Any deviation from law or convention is moral or immoral to the extent that it fails to conform to the convention. For example, if a taxicab's meter is required by law to be correct as to mileage within 2 percent, but a certain taxicab

owner insists that his meter be correct to within 1 percent, then he
is acting in the direction the morality dictates. If, however, a taxi
driver speeds up the clock apparatus for standing time so that it
registers 2 percent faster than it ideally should, he is acting against
the direction of morality. This is our view, even if the law gives him
a 2 percent margin of error, for the error leeway allowed is greater
than his clock is capable of. In a greater sense, three-martini lunches
are immoral if (by intent or fact) they constitute a substitute for
such market standards as price, quality, conditions of contract, etc.
In our view, morality is not related to adherence to convention and
law. *Deviation* from law and convention is the relevant notion.

Justice is personal. We suggest that just behavior is related to what
the recipient of action feels he is entitled to. The entitlement generally
is socially conditioned, but may not be in all cases. If the market rate
of wages is $5 per hour for a given skill rate, an employee of that
category may feel cheated at $5 if the firm employing him has the
reputation of being very profitable, or of being a high wage firm.
If a person is paid less than what he considers his due reward, he
may view it as an injustice, and it may possibly be immoral by our
definition. Should a firm pay less than the conventional or legal
minimum rate, the firm is, in our definitional view, acting with
moral implication. The inefficient job seeker preferring a job, even
below the minimum rate of pay, to unemployment might be satisfied and feel no injustice. Thus justice in the first instance is a highly
personal view. When the observer comes into the picture, he is sometimes hard pressed to distinguish between the moral and the just.
The implications of deviation from the law or convention are not
always easy to decipher.

Ethical behavior, in our definition, has both a just and a moral
content. Where justice is done, the recipient of an act feels the reward to be on the plus side of his perception of what he deserves.
Morality, too, is a deviation from a standard, this time a legal or
conventional standard. Ethics is the consideration of both the just
and the moral.

But a moment's reflection will suggest the narrowness and possible sterility of the general view expressed above. This view would seem
to join moral and just behavior to determine ethical behavior. Such a
conception would be valid only if the parties at ultimate interest
were both the immediate actor and the recipient. In truth, other
parties have interests that may be more important than the effects

on doer and doee. An action, in our opinion, can be considered as just, moral, and ethical only if the realistic implications are considered.

A might consider as a just wage what B pays him. Yet that wage (above the market) may upset the whole labor market; if A is in a class of workers all paid above the market, the effects on employment, labor peace, output, etc., may outweigh the justice and morality accorded A. Legislation designed to alleviate the plight of minorities or assist urban areas, or policies designed to curb inflation and improve employment, may have complex but, on the net, injurious effects on those for whose benefit the actions were undertaken, as well as for other groups and institutions.[7]

Examples of the failure of government intervention in the operation of the market are on the tips of the tongues and pens of those devoted to the neoclassical paradigm. But other examples can just as easily be cited to show that interventions in market operations were, on the net, socially beneficial; or where not so beneficial as they might have been, did really improve the well being of the society. Social Security, as bad as it is, is generally held to be better than no social security. Workman's Compensation has its flaws, but few indeed would want to destroy the institution. Market activism by the state has in many instances been considered socially beneficial, in the light of the ideology and values of the time. Trade unionism, public registration of certain types of securities issues, laws of conspiracy in matters affecting commerce, and the idea of the regulation of public utilities, to name only a few interventionist modes, are in our opinion defensible from a public policy point of view. The ethics of general economic behavior are complex because government and public behavior are implied as well as the firm's. We shall limit the discussion to the firm's behavior. What seem to be determining are ideologies.

How to bring to accord consumer ideal welfare and producer initiative is, of course, a most difficult task, one which is not likely to be solved to everyone's satisfaction. But equally complex are the intraconsumer and intraproducer conflicts of interests. Social solutions are generally second best, so a set of ideal ethical precepts is never likely to be realized; for particular justice and morality rarely if ever achieve complete legitimation.

Our major concern is with the ethical consideration of business behavior. The spectrum of business behavior may conveniently be divided into three sectors:

1. The firm deals with an individual or other entity whose economic power and authority are markedly below that of the firm.

2. The firm operates in a market of purchase and sale where the economic forces and power of the firm, whether large or small, are not entirely compelling. The firm is constrained by the competition of the market, or the competition of alternative supplies and demands constraining the economic power of the firm. For example, General Motors is not only constrained by its American and foreign competitors, it is also constrained by consumers and suppliers.

3. The firm, through advertising, lobbying, or other forms of behavior, makes attempts to affect, control, or influence the social conventions and laws. Such actions may include advertising, attempts to influence legislation, and trade associations preparing codes of conduct for their communicants.

A firm or business is usually a complex organization. Power and authority to initiate and control behavior are often diffuse. Responsibility however, ultimately, perhaps legally, rests with a board or committee of persons who act through a smaller group, often a single person. We shall call the small group or the individual with the authority to act *the manager.* By personalizing the concept of management we are suggesting that responsibility and authority are centralized. But most actions take place without the knowledge, and hence specific approval, of the manager. Actions undertaken without specific approval are not usually disapproved, if they are routine or based on delegated authority. Such actions we define as administrative. In general, administration is the exercise of derived power.

This concept of management and the firm is different from the simple mechanism of economic theory[8] in which the firm reacts to the market situation, originating nothing, improvising nothing, just being a naturalistic mechanism. Our firm, on the contrary, originates, plans, weighs, improvises, and administers. These and other functions are particularities of a given firm. Administration is the internal control of business subject to the general direction of the manager.

Management, then, consists of more than putting out fires set by administration or not put out by administration. Management is more than administering a frictionless program. And our definition of management does not lie between these extremes.

Business leaders of great repute are generally known for their creativity. They are people who see problems that are hidden or, if seen, are considered, by lesser minds, intractable. For leaders the problems are hemmed in by plans and ideas, and the results are often solutions to the problems. Those who clearly see and attack the issues are business leaders. Henry Ford's name comes to mind at once, but Giannini in banking, Durant in putting together General Motors, are also types of leaders of repute. The successes of Watson with IBM, Linowitz with Xerox, Walt Disney, and Henry Kaiser, to name only a few, are successes of creativity. To be sure, their administrations probably were efficient, and threatening fires were put out, but the essence of their successes were ideas, novelty and hard work.

Management, as we define it, is creative. Administration is conventional. The successful administrator (verging on the role of manager) may also make rules that accomplish ends; but administration essentially holds the world together. It conserves and operates rather than creates.

The manager, on the other hand, is a restless soul. His focus is the unusual, the untried, the hidden, the future. His conception of the world is not conventionally systematic. Leading and pushing the firm (the administrators) toward new ways of doing things is sometimes called strategy making. In a realistic sense, strategies are guesses or intuitions about problems whose dimensions are not known and whose solutions are untried. A problem that is not defined and experienced is only surmised.

The manager, then, contemplating and trying to structure the unstructured, is concerned not only with the internal world of the firm, but also with the external world or worlds in which the firm operates. Acceptability to both the internal and external environments is an essential ingredient in any policy. Acceptability to both internal and external environments is the stuff of business ethics.

Particular modes of conduct and behavior that satisfy some ideal of goodness are often the substance of ethical or moral discussion. Some writers view their moral structures as seamless and all-encompassing. Our view is less general and more pragmatic. We are concerned with developing a moral or ethical structure that explains the limits of moral or ethical behavior. Moral and ethical are often used as synonyms. However we shall make a distinction, which often is slight. Moral in our use means acting beyond the requirement of convention. Ethics adds to moral behavior the consideration of justice. If my recollection is correct, the late T. V. Smith once made that distinction in conversation. Behavior is moral if it is acceptable to some value system and is a deviation from merely required behavior. Moral behavior is limited to a defined and given arena of concern. Whatever universe of discourse is given is the area of concern. Each model, each universe of discourse, tends to have its own moral and ethical characteristics.

A single actor, such as a firm, can be treated as an entity or as a complex of parts. For the firm, the adjustment of the parts—for example, production, personnel, and advertising—to each other to produce a harmonious relationship is a sign of a well functioning system. We normally do not use the word moral (or ethical) to describe such harmony, but we might, since each part (and pre-sumably, at the lowest denominator, each person) is providing services that exceed the expectations of each other part.

In fact, harmony is rare. Someone always has a gripe—some un-expected event, a late shipment, the poor quality of inputs, some-thing untoward, exogenous to the firm or any one of its depart-ments, always happens. Disharmony is the rule, and disharmony must be converted to harmony. Correction of disharmony is the administra-tive function. So much for the internal need for extraordinary be-havior, usually by minor officials, lesser management. The great policy issues of the firm are planning and adjusting to the realities of the environment, or controlling the environment.

In a general way, each entity, as an area of concern, has a changing set of goals. To the degree that the goals are achieved (or over-achieved) and rewarded, the members of the firm or its managerial head feel that justice has been done. Insofar as the firm satisfies or exceeds the expectations of other related entities (firms, buyers, suppliers) in their areas of concern, morality is accomplished and moral behavior has been exhibited. Where morality and justice occur simultaneously, ethics is the result. Such equilibria are serendipitous.[9]

But in the reality of living, rarely do all the actors and recipients feel justice has been done, and so they assign an immorality or in-justice to those they are dealing with. Then justice and morality are not coexistent, and ethics is not the result. Approximate justice and approximate morality give approximate ethics.

An entity, a manager, whose actions are not well received may ex-plain his behavior by arguing that it was indeed *justified* and legiti-mated by practice. If the recipient of an act feels that justice was not done him, the perpetrator of the act may argue that the act was normal or conventional—that is, within acceptable limits—and hence should be considered just. The actor tends to subsume justice in convention.

The rules of justice, hence morality, differ for different institutions. A government has a duty to defend itself by being militarily prepared. Such preparation is not constrained only by money costs. A firm has the duty (goal) to make profits and stay in business. If, as necessarily occurs in a free enterprise economy, the government places orders for defense equipment with a firm, the rules of the government are not the same as the rules for the firm. Either some modus vivendi must be arranged to allow each to conduct its affairs in some agreed fashion (e.g., subsidies, cost overruns, extraordinary quality control), or a new government business entity must be created or invented. Either adjustment obviously requires managerial creativity and a novel set of rules concerning just and moral behavior, and an ethical result.

A firm operating in foreign lands may well be caught in a conflict of ideologies, laws, and conventions. To require adherence to ideological ways that are alien to the foreign culture but approved in the United States might amount to moral imperialism. Furthermore, loss of business because the conventions of a foreign host are not respected might be costly to the firm, the United States, the foreign country, and so on. A solution would be to prepare a code of international conduct, have it approved by the appropriate governments, and work up a supranational enforcement agency. The present trial by press and congressional exposure is not an effective way to control doing business in the less developed countries.

In a general way, we can distinguish among behavior patterns and incentives in a firm dealing (1) with an individual or few individuals, (2) with other firms as in a market, and (3) with industries, courts, legislators, academics, or organized interest groups to decide on public policy. In each separate area of concern different concepts of justice, morality, and ethics are involved.

At the minimal extreme—the power of the firm (the manager) in dealing with an individual, or a few individuals—the inequality of power and authority can be equalized by generosity. At the maximal extreme—public policy making—horse trading or compromise are the generally used tools of adjustment. Somewhere in the middle, where a rough equality of power and authority occur in the impersonality of the marketplace, adherence to rule should be the ideal. Failure to adhere to rules tends to create new rules which have not passed through the crucible of legitimation by all the affected, and indirectly affected, parties. There is a danger in permitting social policy to be made by a firm, no matter how great the firm's reputation for social virtue. The study of ethics is (or should be) largely the study of the implications of behavior.

While the bare bones argument we present is primarily directed toward business, it has general application. The social rules for affirmative action, urban renewal, Social Security, military expenditures, or what not, which are legislated, should be compromises that are agreeable in a technical as well as just and moral—that is ethical— sense, to those concerned. In major social problems or major economic and business problems (e.g., foreign competition, employment), the involved parties are not only those directly affected. Control of steel prices and output are not only the concern of the steel industry. Urban renewal affects more than inner city inhabitants and downtown merchants. The implications of behavior are usually, in our opinion, more significant than the behavior undertaken in the first instance.

The argument suggests that ethical behavior is aberrant behavior, deviating from normal, conventional, or institutional behavior in the direction ideology considers good. Evil behavior is such deviation in the conventional direction considered bad.

One immediate query arises from this assertion. Are good and bad, as directions or tendencies, merely conventional? The best approach one can take to this (ideological) question is to try to evade it. Good and bad do seem to be conventional but many, perhaps most, significant meanings of these words have a wide commonality over time and place. Loyalty, concern for the weak, honesty—indeed many of the abstractions of goodness—make almost as much sense to the fifteenth-century Western mind as to the twentieth. Many social virtues we list are more respected as "in-group" ideals in dealing with outsiders. As time runs its course and barriers are broken down, the moral distinctions between insiders and outsiders probably (desirably) diminishes. Conflicting ideas of morality, justice, and ethics make social and economic intercourse most difficult. The applicability of general concepts is probably wider in more secular and accessible societies than in more religious and isolated societies.

Rationality and a consideration of the implications of behavior are more in accord with the former; devotion and duty more implied in the latter. If this contention is sound, ethical, moral, and just behavior is aberrant in that each requires more than convention demands.

Aberrant behavior may be suspect if the effects are to disrupt the social mechanism. The million-dollar gift of food by Mr. Hearst to save his daughter Patty from the ire of her captors may be viewed as an unethical act, insofar as the poor and society were concerned. Patty, to be sure, may have benefited, but the market mechanism and the welfare food distribution mechanism were injured, the hopes of the poor dashed, and petty thieves and bully boys given a field day. Patty's captors may have expected these disruptive results, but their ethical concepts were so abnormal as to deny them a moral or just status. Technically the operation made little sense, and so was neither operational nor (perhaps therefore) ethical.

A deeper evaluation of behavior, whether at the individual, market, or social-planning level, however, is generally more difficult to make than in the example given above.

The effect of any action is rarely limited to the particular event. Actions have a way of triggering other actions, thus changing the environment. When Keynes offered a paradigm of the investment multiplier, it was an invitation for economists to proliferate the idea. The implications of multipliers for economic behavior may well be more significant over time and on other processes than the market action initially being analyzed.

The total effects of a change in the supply of money, or a government deficit, or a new minimum wage, may appear a year or more from the initial time of the event, and in behavior seem only distantly related to the action in question. An awareness of this complex, hidden, subtle web of interconnections appears in the new interest in externalities, which Professor Pigou talked about early in the century. Now we are aware, one might say painfully aware, of the social implications of the behavior of industry, implications which go beyond economic considerations.[10]

So, in general, a deviation from normal conventional behavior may only seem to solve, with a moral and just flavor, a particular problem. The very act of subverting the market may be a signal that the traditional institutions are not performing as they are supposed to.

Ethical behavior is rare, and occurs when deviations from the usual and conventional do not carry in their wake hidden or obscure results which, although hidden and obscure, plague the society and/or the doers of good and the recipients of such behavior. There is no substitute for analysis to evaluate, in advance, both substantive and ethical behavior. There is great possibility of public or social disadvantage should firms unilaterally decide issues or public policy. The amount of air pollution a firm generates cannot reasonably be a decision of the firm alone. Or two or more firms cannot be allowed to decide on a market or price policy without possibly endangering the society and its markets. Policy, public policy, should be a compromise of many interest groups if functionality is to be preserved. The complexity of market issues probably implies the desirability of fairly general laws articulating social policy and then allowing discretionary leeway to the courts. The latter has evolved; the former approach has not become deeply imbedded in the ideology.

The pressure and pull of technology, various conceptions of self and social interest, and other exogenous forces impinge on the ideological bundle that societies develop. The potential for new or not fully legitimated behaviors is the mark of a dynamic society. Laissez faire–laissez passer, a startling legitimation in the seventeenth and eighteenth centuries, gives way to the ideal of restriction and intervention to assist in achieving the good life at the end of the twentieth century. The ideals of ends and means being technically and uniquely related, with neither justifying the other, is not satisfying. It is as if means and ends are uniquely part of the same continuum. But alternative means usually are available. And ends themselves are ideologically legitimated, often independently of means. The web of legitimation, ethics, justice, and morality is multidimensional and not of a seamless construction.

2

THE MANAGEMENT TRAP
A Simple Model of the Firm

People tend to do what they do best, and enjoy doing what they do best. This is the essence of the activity trap. The usual, riskless, ritualistic task which promises success is for most people more attractive than the risky, novel, unusual job. The activity trap is found at every level of management and decision making. It is the rare decision maker, manager, or administrator, who searches out problems, who risks defeat because the challenge is exciting. The rare manager is the successful one.

The activity trap is also a management trap. People do what they do best, and what they know how to do.[1]

The business firm can be divided into compartments whether or not the parts exist on some flow chart or organizational chart. The marketing people do their thing, and are managed into some coordinate relation to the production department, which in turn is coordinated with the accounting department and so on across the board. Coordination is one managerial function. Within the department too, coordination occurs often as ritual or routine, as well as with thought and insight. How papers are routed, forms filled out, and reports made or requested are often routines, sometimes useful, sometimes merely time consuming and boring.

The fuss of persistent rearrangement of duties and functions, of frequently changing product lines and ways of selling the product, of often altering plans for growth and retrenchment, in very short periods of time, would upset the balances and tempo of the firm.

Constant change would be disruptive to any organization; expectation of constant change leads to fear of change. Yet no change at all, or no change when its need is indicated, would be the death knell of an organization. Some changes in structure, procedure, and products go on all the time in the large firm, but the changes are usually not sufficiently large to affect the nature or spirit of the institution.

We can look upon the business firm in the short run as a stable institution, or as a "black box." Information comes in, is analyzed, and is transmuted to behavior.[2] The behavior may be entirely within the firm or it may have an outreach into the environment of the firm. If a customer orders steel of certain specifications, he expects his order to be honored and he expects to receive steel of the given specifications in a reasonable, i.e., expected, period of time. If a company exaggerates or lies about its planned product in order to forestall sales of a competitor, the firm may be sued and judged guilty of restraint of trade.

If we assume that business is a self-contained unit, we must further assume that it exists in an environment. The most obvious environment for a particular firm is the competition of the market. By "competition" we do not mean a market which is a model of the pure and perfect competition of economic theory. All we mean is that other firms are selling substitute commodities which, from a viewpoint of price, service, and technology, might satisfy the needs of buyers, and hence might attract them from one firm to another.[3]

So far as the firm is concerned, from this narrow view, the environment is the competitive surrounding. Now, the competitive firm becomes a little more complex in its behavior if into such a simple environment is thrust some governmental action or inhibition. Such government intervention might be with regard to ecological pollution control, minimum wages, or new taxes. Nongovernment-generated changes are in consumer demand or the offering of substitute goods. Then the firm clearly has to react, more or less drastically, depending on the severity of the market change and its own internal adjustments to meet the new circumstance. The firm does this by advertising, by retraining its labor force, by lobbying for protective legislation, by developing and using research and development, etc., so as to improve its competitive and market stance. Or it may merge with another company. Bankruptcy is an ultimate adjustment.

The black box (the firm) is a mystery. "Mystery" is an old word (which is, in modern French, *metier*) which simply means a calling, a job, or a skill. The mysteries of business are the details of accounting, advertising, research and development, personnel, management, marketing, and all the other disciplines in which a firm engages. By themselves these mysteries were merely disciplines or ordering modes of behavior. Grouped together within a firm, the disciplines make possible the ongoingness of the firm, including the reactions of the firm to the environment. Indeed the disciplines, taken together, and given tasks to perform, are the firm.

To the outside world, to an observer in the environment, the black box—the firm—is a unity. The farther away we are from General Motors or the 3M Company, the more unified and coordinated seem the actions of these two firms. Indeed we can almost personify them; the company becomes a person, a complete thing. The closer however one comes to General Motors or to 3M, the more one is aware of the divisions and the departments, the minor functions which make up the companies.

The people within the black box are used to, and understand, the mechanism in the box. The people outside tend to see it as a gestalt, a totality, unless they have previous knowledge of the company structure. The people who inhabit the black box tend to move safely within it, creating no outside ripples, tending to look mainly inward and rarely outward to the environment, unless looking out is their particular responsibility. Black box people tend to be those who are caught in the activity trap, and who often tend to see new problems and procedures as destructive of ritual.

But the firm—the black box—is always subject to impingement by its external and internal environments. Threats are negative—that is, threats of destruction, loss of business, or in general, new constraints which limit the firm in its search for persistence via profits. Or indications may be positive—that is to say, opportunities for expansion, assurances of persistence and profits.

Both negative and positive impingements are challenges. The positive ones tend to require, in addition to all the other traits of those facing such challenges, courage and drive. The negative ones tend to require as special traits an understanding of how existing resources can be rearranged to keep the black box afloat. Growth, profitability may be available to the firm, but only if the managers have insight, are willing to take risks, and in general, know something about the nature of the environment. All impingements, negative or positive, are challenges. How they are seen by the manager is the issue. As soon as the manager understands the significance of the impingement, and begins to figure out what to do, he has overcome the activity trap.

For the manager endowed with entrepreneurial skills, the capacity and willingness to take on new problems, the firm is a system for information gathering, analysis, synthesis, and then putting in place an action program. The details of administration take over from there. Details are typically left in the hands of competent technicians. The essential challenge to the entrepreneur and the skilled manager is to see how the firm can maneuver itself in the environment, so as to achieve a set of goals without disrupting the internal anatomy of the firm, except by choice and plan. But in the manager's calculations, notions of justice, morality, and ethics must intrude themselves because morale rests on morality, and furthermore managers must retain their self-respect.[4]

Ideally the skill of the manager is to coordinate purpose and behavior so as to secure a harmony of purposes for the firm, while at the same time having a vision of new purposes. A role of the skilled manager is to spring the activity trap, never to get himself caught in it, and constantly to take advantage of the realities of the world. This implies maintaining an *esprit de corps* within the firm, and foreseeing and controlling governmental and other interventions.

In the dynamic operation of an industry such a policy of anticipation may help to soften the effects of forthcoming regulation by removing negative effects over a period of time and through technical innovation. For example, anticipation of future safety regulation has possibly motivated automotive manufacturers to develop safety devices and begin their manufacture in advance of laws compelling them to do so. In almost all cases safety devices were available to consumers as optional accessories in advance of any regulation requiring them. Since the corporation is primarily concerned with futurity and perpetuity, it shares with government a fundamental interest in consumer and social welfare.

The skilled manager, in his high role, then seeks always to adjust his firm to the environment, and the environment to his firm. To be sure, he is concerned with the ongoingness of the firm, with the appropriate harmony of the various divisions and sectors, but he is more concerned, in the usual situation, with the place of the firm in the environment. This is why "share of the market" is such a significant measure, and why social acceptance is so important.

The manager sees the future as history, which is another way of saying he must anticipate the changes in the relevant environment and set in motion adaptive changes within the firm. This is the first step. The second step is to change or try to change the external environment so as to make it more congenial.

The manager obviously does not rely solely for his vision and his decisions on either micro economic or macro economic theory. These may be rationalizations of a decision. The manager uses all the analytic resources at his disposal, always weighing costs and returns.

It is the great decisions which are strategic because there are no routines by which to make them. Obviously not many of the decisions of a firm in the course of a week, a month, a year are great strategic decisions. And just as obviously the skilled manager—a person with insight, responsibility—sets the stage for the decisions. Such decisions may appear routine to his colleagues and competitors, but in truth they often do represent breaks with the past. For example, the decision of American automobile companies to emphasize smaller, lighter cars was not made quickly. Indeed government and consumer groups complained bitterly that the industry was slow in its changing over from the so-called gas guzzlers to compacts. Yet this was a strategic decision which could not be made quickly, since the technological, administrative, and marketing considerations required a great deal of thought and planning, and so a great deal of time. The failure of the Edsel is, in a sense, offset by the success of the Pinto. It is the uninformed and careless who argue that business is generally inept and foolish in its market decisions. Decisions are frequently forced on industry by the facts of its environment, e.g., the pollution problem. At first industry may resist the inevitable, a foolish stance. But the resistance is often more in the minds of the critics than in the minds of the decision makers. They simply do not know precisely how to go about doing what they have to do. Nor can industrial change always be accomplished quickly.

This discussion suggests the question of the limits of management. Can a manager be so bright, so insightful, so reflective, so activistic that there are no limits, except the legal ones, to his behavior, to the growth of his firm, to the conglomeration of a number of firms under his tutelage? Pretty obviously the limit to the size of the firm and to the complexity of a business organization is the skill of management and the size of the market. While there are great variations in managerial skills and competence, no manager can work more than twenty-four hours a day, even though a synergistic team may. Nor will the staff be the dedicated geniuses our hypothetical paragon of a manager is. It seems fair to argue that a significant constraint on the size of a business organization is the manager and his skills. The size of the market, as Adam Smith pointed out, limits the division of labor, or in our language the technology. But market size and the number and size of competitors are also of interest to the Anti-Trust Division. Thus human capacity, market size, and public policy all interact in affecting the size of a firm.

Managers must do what no one else is equipped to do. "Chance, love, and logic" all play their role in his decisions. Love is the affections people have for each other—the human relations aspect of decisions. Logic, in this context, means the capacity of people to analyze and synthesize the environments by models and information. Chance is the property of the environment which eludes analysis. This is not to say that an analysis of a chance event is not assumed to be possible. The world is assumed to be ordered, but this assumption does not automatically tell what the order is. We assume the environment is ordered, but we often act as if chance were a prominent feature. The manager is the person who can reduce chance to order and probability, to a greater extent than other people can.

In all this interplay of chance, love, and logic, the manager, as the brain of the firm, is judged by a measure which is quite different from those which usually quantify success or failure. The manager, and hence the firm, is judged by public opinion, by the degree to which the action is in accord with the morality of the time and place. Unacceptable behavior is not long tolerated.

In the previous observations we suggested that the skilled manager, engaged in managing a firm, is a person who explores the environment external and internal to the firm to find and anticipate problems. The manager seeks institutional effectiveness and efficiency, and also sets the goals of improvement. The interest in people (employees) *qua* people is unofficial. The firm only incidentally tries to improve people. That is not its function, although making people happier and better is, of course, a noble calling. Making people happier as a means for making the firm more effective is an ideal never to be neglected. Making people happier for the sake of making people happier is a dangerous game, and superfluous for a manager or firm.

Goals of the firm always assume profitability, explicitly or implicitly, and perpetuity, i.e., a persistence and improvement of the net worth of the firm. Profitability is an operating concept, net worth, a static or balance sheet concept. The two are obviously not the same, although over time they are related. Salability, another implicit goal, is a more persistent measure of the ongoing value of the firm to its owners, and hence to others desiring to acquire the firm. It is the market value placed on a firm, the actual value in a sale, not the "book value," and derives from profitability. Perpetuity means permanence of income and hence capital value.

The value of the firm to owners or buyers requires that the firm have a moral acceptance in the market where its product is sold, and by those (including government) with the power to destroy or restrain the firm. In this regard, we make a distinction between legitimate and illegitimate business. The Mafia cannot directly sell shares in itself on the open market. Indirectly, of course, it may be able to secure financing.

Cause and effect, or means and ends, are common ways to analyze relationships. But to understand the nature of an event or a social entity as an institution or person, we often define the event, institution, or person in terms of phenomena we have had experience with, or on which there is a common understanding. Analogy and metaphor are parts of explanation. We often speak of the life cycle of a product. The product grows old and without oomph just as people do. We speak of arthritic firms as if firms have arms and legs to suffer the ravages of arthritis. We speak of some firms as being lean and hungry. Such words are dramatic and may invoke images in the mind of the reader or listener.

All analogies are dangerous, because things are what they are and not what something else is. Analogy is, in a sense, a variety of poetry. But analogies are interesting and suggestive. It is difficult, almost impossible, to explain a phenomenon newly experienced in terms only of itself and its parts. It also may be dull to do so. Analogy, metaphor, "as if," generally help us communicate. To be sure, there always is a danger in "as if," but without it we may lose the opportunity even to try to make our views known. Brute facts or so-called logical functions are hard to define except by "as if," by analogy. But it is easier to define a corporation for a person who knows about social and economic institutions than for a person whose social knowledge is vague and naturalistic.

The firm—that is, a legally constituted agency organized to do business—may be seen as a hierarchical structure made up of people and capital performing certain functions. We might have defined the firm around mechanical devices—that is, technology, as an engineer might easily do. We prefer to see the firm as an idea-information agency, with people as the realities which are motivated by ideas and perform so as to realize the ideas and satisfy the ideals of the firm. Information is the motive force; approval and acceptability by owners and the society, the output. The complexity of a firm, with its bundle of goals and its array of means, can be defined differently for the several frames of reference in which it may operate. In a general sense, since all firms need information to determine behavior and ends, we can look at the firm as an information system. Signals are received, transposed to information in the light of need, and actions are generated.[5]

The purposes of the firm, we suggest, are conditioned by the constraints placed upon its possible actions. Purposes or goals are selections and are not automatically given. Means too are chosen, chosen in the light of information, goals, and technology. The choice element in ends and means is why abstract theory so often must be particularized before a manager can use it. What one cannot do limits the choice of what one can do.

The policies and practices of the firm are the results of ideas of people, legitimated over time and by approval of managerial authority. Here is the nub of the question. Policies and practices once devised are the constraints placed upon firm behavior. Firms really do not behave or misbehave (in spite of the current interpretation of the Fourteenth Amendment of the Constitution). *People* behave, as individuals, or act in concert. The constraints on their action are in part imposed by "brute fact," by the realities of life, and in part by their agreement or acceptance of appropriate behavior.

All hell breaks loose when constraints attempt to control employee behavior outside the confines of the firm or in petty ways within the firm. IBM has or had the reputation of being unduly restrictive of the off-the-job personal behavior of its employees. Once at a conference of IBM engineers I was inundated for two days by complaint, criticism, and contempt for what was seen as IBM pettiness. I had no solution, nor indeed any connection with the company. The vehemence of the complaints by middle management was bewildering to me.[6]

A person who finds the job onerous may always quit. A manager who is driven by demons, or who is a high achiever, might want his staff or workforce to operate in an extraordinary fashion. It is needless to point out that the response to such managerial leadership is to get rid of the manager before he destroys the morale of his own staff and superiors.

The viable firm, insofar as possible, gives leeway to people to behave, to experiment, and to be themselves. The office party, the suggestion box, conversations among employees and between staff people and manager about what might be done and what is being done, are information sharing and the creating of information and ideas. Creativity, if never reined and directed, however, may react against production and organization goals.[7] But on the other hand, if creativity is reined too tightly it may lead to a disgruntled labor force, and even worse, a disinterested labor force, at both the white collar and the blue collar levels. The proper allowance for creativity, of course, is a managerial goal.

The firm is a very complex place with all sorts of ideas, behavioral thrusts, personality considerations, affecting the ongoingness of the institution. These are the fabric of the internal environment.

3

THE FALLACY OF THE RABBLE HYPOTHESIS

A visit to the inner sanctum of a top corporate executive can tell much about how its occupant views the world outside. Long rows of functionaries who prevent the world from entering, deep carpeting to hush the strident noises of the street and the world, all are symptoms of what the top people who decide the firm's policy believe about the outside world. Consciously or not, they view the population at large as disorganized, and as a rabble. Perhaps it is the face of a rowdy picket line shouting through car windows. Perhaps it is a ragtag, denim-clad, aggressive audience at a college speech. It might even be pictured as a lowbrow dolt in an undershirt sitting before a boob tube ripping tops from beer cans, watching some ruffians bash each other over a hundred yards of astroturf.

Management's idea that management must be disliked, or at least be misunderstood by the world at large, is, of course, often a self-fulfilling prophecy. And so is its opposite. People who assume that society, government, students, consumers, and people at large are hostile to business will indeed find them so. People who assume the opposite, will often find *it*.

In truth, the underlying relationship between business and society has a core which is neither adulatory nor deeply hostile. This chapter is a defense of the business system as an adjustive, accommodating institution. It attempts to show that the reduction of social tensions, while difficult and often impossible, is a process which, if worked at, accomplishes the purposes of society. This is a big order for a small chapter. We hope the argument is suggestive.

Business success is not always a bitch goddess; in many cases it is just a bitch. Business in recent years has often been on the defensive. The post-Watergate era of exposure and the resulting cynicism have not generated a happy time for many people and institutions with authority. Big business has often been the object of censure, or at least criticism, in the public eye. Business leaders themselves no longer project the confidence and general, all-purpose sapience they seemed to possess in the 1950s and 1960s—and earlier, in the 1920s.

The post-Watergate scandals of political payoffs, the Lockheed and Penn Central capers, the oil-energy publicity fiasco, Hollywood's chicanery, these and other publicized unwholesome events and innuendos have not made business a revered institution. Government, too, has had its troubles, as have other public institutions such as hospitals, the medical profession, schools, colleges, and science (which wants to fool around with genetics). Even the Nobel Prize Committee has been criticized for having made Milton Friedman sweat out his honor for three or four years because the economic subcommittee in Stockholm did not like Friedman's conservative politics.

No institution seems immune from criticism, even pretty nasty criticism. These years have been called variously the Age of Vulgarity and the Age of Uncertainty. Such titles are apt. But the Age of Criticism also is apt. As a society we seem in the constant process of applying rational criticism to institutions and values which really can not stand up to the particular analytic criticism they are subjected to. The roles of ritual, ethics, and the rationality of irrational behavior are not given proper weight or function in superficial criticism.

The assumption or assertion that business management is in conflict with the rest of society is, in our opinion, a mistake about the nature of American society. A concern with ethics, with justice and morality, is deep in the roots of society. That all its members must agree on The Ethic, on a homogeneous set of values, is a view alien to a society which prides itself on its diversity of view. But diversity of view does not necessarily imply conflict. Some irreducible differences may be and, in our opinion, are vital elements in a lively social order. *"Vivere pugnare est,"* carved into the foundations of Houston Hall at the University of Pennsylvania, may go a bit far. But to live is to be lively, and liveliness requires differences among people. On the other hand, no society could exist if it did not have broad social agreement on some principles, and an ability to compromise on others. America, if it is other things, is also the land of compromise.

Business often views itself as the heart of society. The heart is a pump which supplies the body (economic, in this case) with the means of supporting life. But would life exist without arms, legs, kidneys, eyes, and lungs? All are parts of the body, and each performs a function. If legs could speak, they undoubtedly would make a case for the importance of locomotion. This kind of argument, as a prelude for special treatment or respect, is neither rewarding nor convincing. The body economic is a collection of interactive parts, and for varying purposes some parts are more important than others. The body is functional, with functions focused on varying goals.

We may assume business is an institution of major significance in securing the livelihood of the total society. An artist, a scientist, and a plumber might reasonably be expected to hold different views as to the relative importance of institutions, each one reflecting the part of society he knows best. What would the world be without indoor plumbing or symphony orchestras? While the society does fairly well, in general, its high marks are more in comparison to the past than to the unrealized potential of the present. The poor, uneducated, unhappy, stunted, stultified are still with us—classes and individuals. The air is dirty and water is scarce and often polluted, "energy" is a bogeyman word, and honesty is still an unrealized ideal. Life is better than it was, but it still is not good for many of the world's billions. How good is the potential is a question we tend to evade, but it always haunts the powerful in high places.

American society and world society have not earned high marks as to acceptability. Maybe this is why we stress output indices and a high standard of living rather than the quality and distribution of income. Yet we know acceptability implies satisfaction and is what the ancients called harmony. We know that harmony and acceptability can be heightened by a dose of conflict. One really cannot win without the threat of losing. One cannot accomplish unless the goal may also be lost. Modern music and art generally recognize this, and tragic plays are always taken more thoughtfully than comedies and farces. The human comedy has not been much of a comedy since the Garden of Eden.

Maybe failure of the public to recognize these truths leads advertisers to stress the ease of their product in use. The school of learn-to-play-the-piano without lessons, practice, or trying, how to do this or that, or become this or that, without really putting oneself out, is a come-on for the less socially skilled and sophisticated. We all know that such a view, in the specific, is a false one, but we all fantasize about success without effort, if only for a change. On the other hand, tools and techniques which make meaningful jobs easier are of a different order. Here the task is eased but not made into a sure thing. Life without effort and risk would be dull indeed. If all the world could paint a Rembrandt, Rembrandt paintings would not be very exciting.

Business is bathed in uncertainty. Practitioners of business would enjoy certainty only until it began to pall, which would be quickly. "Challenge" is a word often used by businessmen to justify their interest.

Business behavior, and hence the degree of public approval, varies with what is expected of business. The expectations of buyers, sellers, governments, employees, owners, and technologists are not constant. Rather, they interact with each other, and also with the forces from outside the market or even the society. The interactions are the forces of competition, and competition is bargaining in a market. The results, the stability which is sought in a free market, comes out of compromise and is never achieved for long. In a monopolistic situation stability derives from market power, the opposite of compromise.

Thermodynamics has no counterpart in the social world. The Third Law tells us that the energy of the physical world becomes increasingly unavailable for work, that the equalization of heat (and energy) is constantly occurring among different bodies. In other words, there is a cosmic tendency toward the equilibrium of entropy.

In the social world, as we see it, energy, the capacity and requirement to perform, to adjust, to change, is *increasing,* at least in our era.[1] The tendency to inaction and randomness is in no way a mark of modern society. Indeed it is as if the opposite generally is true. An event in Africa or Asia Minor may affect the political and social life of the United States, the Soviet Union, and the whole world. A tough winter in the North American wheat belt may change the Soviet Union's foreign policy and the price of caviar. The world is interrelated politically, artistically, economically, and in every other way. Social energy grows as the problems of society grow. But the interrelations and interactions do not lead to equilibrium. Just try to make some sense out of the gyrations of interest rates, of the stock market, or of the labor market, without having recourse to the most complex hypotheses.

Nationally, business, government, and social institutions generally do not seem to be moving to a stable equilibrium either with each other or within their own confines. Rather, great sections of world and national society seem to be moving away from stability while other sections may be mutually adjusting. Certainly equilibrium or stability over any extended time is not a general characteristic, even in such freely adjustive phenomena as style in clothes, art, politics, and technology.

Much of business behavior is restricted by law, technology, and convention. But there always is a slack in the constraints which permits adjustment to exogenous or new events. Exogenous forces impinge upon institutions, business and others, and so induce novel behavior and structural changes. Style, expectation, and public opinion (a rough name for a major part of convention) affect business decisions just as cost and returns do. And business is judged by owners, buyers, and the general public, in part, on how well it adapts to the market forces and to all the other novel, unexpected forces which are brought to bear on business. The social world abhors a static equilibrium as nature abhors a vacuum.

With change and adjustment built into the business system, just and moral behavior too must accommodate. Organization and technological change often create new issues and require new forms of behavior which are considered just and moral. Those most intimately connected with business—owners, employees, buyers—each in his own special, selfish way, want *justice* from business. Those less intimately connected want *morality* from business. And business—that is, the manager, the responsible head—wants to stay out of trouble, provide justice and morality for others, plus justice for himself and his "people." This is like walking a tightrope on a broken leg. It is possible but difficult.

The justice and morality seekers (who may sometimes seem like justice and morality freaks to the manager) may form coalitions among themselves. Ralph Nader is the current American prophet of this phenomenon. Managers beset by hostile and varying pressures, too, seek coalition, often with the trade unions, or with government (the basis of payoffs?), or with competitors. The last we call conspiracy, and it is anathema in law, as it should be.

The critics, too, form coalitions. Blacks may team up with consumers, until finally their interests diverge. Consumers try to influence legislation, or get a personage close to the Oval Office. Buyers may conspire to boycott large firms. This is possibly a violation of law, but as such it is harder to prove than is a union of sellers, which has been known to occur. The whole marketplace is in a flux of behavior and attitude, and the government is inevitably drawn in as a protagonist, or as a regulator and adjudicator. The point is that the business system is in a flux seeking to accommodate incompatible views. Compromise is the short-lived result. The system lives; it is not frozen. Heat is an aspect of energy.

But justice and morality—what one thinks he should get and what one thinks should be done to others—are ever present in big decisions. They are not the means, nor the particular ends of social and private action. But justice and morality are the motives and legitimations of behavior and goals. Justice and morality, as ideas and ideals, are significant in business decision making, in spite of protestations by some critics and businessmen.[2]

Within the confines of fairly well delimited areas of activity, the behavior of business managers and administrators is obvious and well ordered. Choices are pretty much predetermined. In routine matters of marketing or accounting, or even in ticklish matters such as collective bargaining or introducing a new product, experience and convention effectively dictate how business should behave. Different contexts of behavior and varying environments require alternate procedures. We suggest that when the confines of business behavior—that is, the appropriate choices—are restricted and defined, the exercise of such choices be called administration rather than management.

To be sure, some role for decision making is always present. The mechanic working on a car rarely has only one way to proceed. The manager of the service shop clearly has more decisions to make than the mechanics, for more alternatives are open to him. And so on up to the president of General Motors or Ford, where the decisions are less and less confined by law, technology, convention, or custom than at the lower levels. Yet choice almost always involves more than mere alternative routines. Good and bad for someone—hence ethics—and thus the implications of behavior, are inevitably, if not always purposively, involved.

The social criticism of business is rarely on a technical basis. After all, what difference does it make to a critical observer if a firm finances itself by debt when the situation called for equity; or if a new model car is ignored by potential buyers? But if an auto firm misrepresents the motors it puts under the hoods of a product line, all hell breaks loose. The issue is not whether the engines "do the job." The issue is the engines were not those which the firm said it supplied. Justice, morality, and ethics, and probably the law, have each been violated. The understandable ignorance of the future on the part of realtors or stockbrokers, or the lack of success of surgeons in improving an inevitably deteriorating condition, are often treated as lapses from morality by those affected, and by others who for one reason or another are interested.

Business may be under a barrage of social criticism (probably not so severe as some business leaders believe). But business, too, can and does criticize its critics. The counter-criticism levied by business against its detractors often is not very effective, nor is it generally taken seriously.

Letters to shareholders about the nature of the world, and of business in general, ultimately are judged by the bottom line of the income statement. Did the firm make money, did the market values of its shares rise, and will it do better? Positive answers to such questions are what the shareholder wants. All else are excuses. To justify behavior as moral, or to attack critics raucously in the public press or in quarterly or annual reports, is generally beside the point. Nor do businessmen often sound ill-mannered and angry. It is as if American businessmen assume that to act with style, with restraint and with decorum is a large ingredient in the legitimation of their behavior. Style is the behavioral manner which invites acceptability, independently of the content of the act being performed. The titans, sometimes called robber barons or worse, included many men of style. Carnegie, J. P. Morgan, Harriman, and in later years Henry Ford, the two Charles (engine and electric) Wilsons, each had a flair for attracting favorable attention, in spite of the adverse criticism they generated.

Latter day business characters are hard to spot in a public setting because business is more and more managed by professional managers, paid hands, if you will. They move about from job to job, often from industry to industry, performing what the public and press often see as arcane rites. Politicians, ball club owners, movie and television stars, and a few scientists have assumed the mantle of style in these days.

C. West Churchman is a philosopher whose philosophizing is directed toward business.[3] His work is, or should be, of powerful interest to those who are concerned with the nature of business behavior. He does have a few conclusions which may clarify our questions on the structure of ethics. Churchman sees business as a process. Among his insights is that the manager, whom he views as essentially a manager of information, has three choices in his vision of reality:

1. The manager can believe that the operations of the world are inherently rational. His goal, therefore, is to clarify his own thinking and model construction so that he can predict what will happen.

2. He can believe that the environment of his concern is essentially not predictable (nonrational). The managerial task then is to build a strong structure so as to be able to manage the inputs from experience. Since the world is not predictable, the manager has a chance of changing it.

3. The manager can believe that events in his environment are episodic, that reality as a continuum is irrelevant. Therefore freedom of action, flexibility of decision, "act, act in the living present," are his ideals of management.

In the realm of moral, just, and hence ethical behavior, an A type of manager charts his course as if he knew the shoals and reefs. The moral conventions and those of justice are treated as givens. Engine Charley Wilson's dictum that "what is good for General Motors is good for America" is an example of moral and ethical certitude rarely matched.

The type B manager tries to make order out of chaos. The steel industry and steel union joined, in 1977, in inducing a government policy of an equalizing import duty on low-priced Japanese steel which hopefully would confer order on a chaotic (declining) market. Yet the steel industry and labor have no qualms about buying imports or selling abroad. The faith in "Buy American" may create a xenophobic moral climate, which for some people becomes the norm.

The type C manager believes that there is no norm, for his purposes. His concern is not with creating one, but rather with taking advantage of the vagaries of public opinion. The ethics or morality of selling a product dangerous to health is of little concern. The moral and just thing to do is sell the product, and let the buyer look after himself. Illegal businessmen fall into this category, but *caveat emptor* is an old adage which has the added legitimation of being in Latin. Has its relevance declined in the modern world?

The two classes of managers A and B may be joined into a single class of planners and assumers of order. The theoretical mind looks for or imposes order in his environment, and then follows a plan or policy respecting that order. The manager B, seeking to construct a general environment in conformity with his experience, structures his world of action. The A manager acts as if order exists.

No manager fits only one of the three possibilities. Under different circumstances and under varying pressures, business leaders adjust their outlooks. But it is fair to assert that some managers have more of one characteristic than another. In differing situations it would not be surprising if conventional behavior had alternative faces. Values and the normal ways of behavior are likely to be different as pressures and problems wax and wane.

The opportunist seizes the day, keeps his eye on the main chance, rolls with the punches—and obeys all the other related clichés. But since his course is not rigidly set, he has the opportunity to, and usually will, improvise and depart from convention more easily than more uptight managers. Hence the opportunist may engage in generous behavior without upsetting his own sense of equilibrium. Opportunism may be displayed at higher levels of behavior (market or social policy), but there the opportunities for personalized, individuated behavior are less, and so generous behavior is more limited.

The policy making attempts of these C persons is often messy. Mafia business leaders are supposed to engage in compromises, but often violently break the conventions until force itself becomes a convention. High flyers in business and finance are often reputed to be generous to their employees, but tough on the competition. Roy Cohen's lawsuits and the Hollywood exposé of 1978 (the Begelman affair) indicate small attachment to generally held moral values.

The planful managers A and B are in a different league. Insofar as their efforts are related to the level of interaction of institutions and persons, or the market level, the opportunity for deviation is less than for their opportunistic colleagues. The moral impulses of the planful conform insofar as convention and law are recognized constraints. Here one may find bureaucracy at its worst. Once after paying a $50 or $100 electric bill by a personal check at the utility office, I tried to cash a $10 check to take my wife to lunch. The clerk was adamantly unwilling to cooperate. Checks are for paying bills, not for cashing. How did the company know I was good for $10? This after accepting my $50 or $100 with a smile! Costless generosity to the customer was not in the rule book. The vice president for personnel of the same utility company agonized for about a year over whether to employ blacks. Not until forced to change his personnel policy did he do so, although he was entirely sympathetic to hiring blacks. The rule book made it difficult, and rule books are not to be changed! Underpay a department store by even 50¢ on a bill, or even worse, overpay the store by that amount! Exchanges of letters costing many dollars, and much frustration, will be required to solve the matter to clerical or computer satisfaction.

Bureaucracy is inherent in any organization, and is a function of size and power vis-à-vis the person or institution being victimized. The manager is often not sensitive to the weight of the bureaucracy he heads. A personal complaint, more likely than not, will be explained by the administrative requirement of bureaucratic weight and ineptness. Ineptness repeated becomes a rule. Some managers see through the bureaucratic maze and do simplify the requirements. They are the geniuses of administration. Too few examples come to mind. Few big banks or companies are callous to big customers.

At the market and policy levels planful managers tend to exercise their ethical purposes by obedience to plan and law. If the plan does not correlate with law, the law may well suffer. The planner can also be very tough if his motivations or nature are ungenerous and mean. Corporate officials who bribe or act in concert with competitors to fix prices or share markets may find meaningful justification in relating their misdeeds to targets and goals which were set. At the policy level, as we have suggested, the greater part of ethics lies in not taking undue advantage of the firm's power, although "undue" is hard to delimit. At the market level, however, ethical behavior seems not so significant as adherence to law and legitimated convention. Rarely can deviation from these constraints be legitimated. The illegal sale of James Joyce's book *Ulysses* in the 1930s, or allowing young men to evade the draft during the Vietnam War, may well turn out to have been important acts of ethical significance. The laws themselves were immoral.

At this high level ethical questions are not usually restricted to a single institution. Many parties' interests are involved. At the policy—which is to say, ideological—level business frustration seems at its very greatest. This view is amply documented by Silk and Vogel.[4]

Silk of the *New York Times* and Vogel of the University of California at Berkeley were invited to meetings of leaders of American business by the Conference Board. Virtually all the firms represented were among the Fortune 500 for manufacturing. Important new contenders were also present. The discussions were centered about profits, ethics, and business leaders' conceptions of the social image and role of business.

According to Silk and Vogel, the burden of the argument seems to be that big business managers are really self-assured tycoons who tell this one to come, and he cometh, and that one to go, and he goeth. At least inside the confines of the firm, where the manager clearly is boss. But insecurity and doubt are also attitudes of the Captains of Industry when concerned with matters outside the spans of control of their offices.

This dual attitude is in accord with our observation that ordinary and difficult problems arising within the scope of the accepted business disciplines can be, and are handled as administrative matters. The sticky issues are those which are not amenable to the routines of administration. However it is not suggested that, in decision making within or outside the firm, individual wisdom, insight, and luck play no role. On the contrary. Gambits with high probability of success are used, but the areas in which they are used are fairly well defined. Experience helps the administrator as well as the manager over the rough spots.

Silk and Vogel suggest that self-assurance is less apparent when the top level manager finds himself in the less well defined area of policy, public or private. With labor leaders and labor generally the manager not only is at his ease, he has at his disposal well trained minions to do the routine work. In the past forty years or so, since NRA days, firms have had more and more frequent bargaining contacts with labor unions, and have spent literally millions of hours in grievance meetings.

We suggest that the area of argument is now well defined by law and convention. College and university courses are taught in collective bargaining and personnel management, executive seminars held, books written. In brief, experience is overwhelming. In reality, if not in law, unions are part of the firm's structure. Romantics, and often the press, stress the conflict relationships between union and management, labor and capital, or bosses and workers. One may add that the romantic view is often expressed by business leaders when making a speech on "The Free Enterprise System" and "How to Keep America Prosperous." Labor leaders giving pep talks on "All We Want Is a Fair Deal" and "What Are We Entitled To" also frequently stress the conflict aspects of labor relations. But speeches of such nature should not be taken too seriously in an analysis of the state of affairs. They are utopian at best, or at worst propaganda statements designed to justify some often unrelated ideological action. The articulated moral issues, or issues of justice, are more likely to be at bottom bargaining or publicity stratagems. Policy is being made, so compromises are being struck. The issues are less concerned with morality and justice than they often appear to be.

When meeting with politicians, or liberals dedicated to saving the physical environment, or consumer groups who feel that they are being somehow ripped off, businessmen seem at a loss, according to Silk and Vogel. And not surprisingly. The area of discussion, the implicit and explicit values, the goals and appropriate means are not agreed upon, nor even well defined. Do the ecologists want safety or "no nukes" presumably because nuclear energy is "unnatural," as well as dangerous? Or are the ecologists really no-growth supporters, viewing energy as an ingredient of economic growth? To most businessmen economic growth is a value which is beyond debate, and energy is a necessity of life. An argument really never occurs because the antagonists are talking at cross purposes. They are creating sound waves, and nothing more.

Yet real technological issues are in the background, issues which require solution from any reasonable point of view. What to do with nuclear waste and how to assure plant safety? Camping on a nuclear site may be exciting, getting arrested romantic, especially if one is sure not to be sent to jail, but the issues are not resolved by such behavior. Similarly quoting the law, which fails to deal with the issue, assuring one and all that safety is built in when all the available information makes such an assertion hard to believe, and avoiding the problem of radioactive waste, is not a morally defensible stance. Morality and ethics are being served by neither side.

It is passing strange that businessmen should, as they often do, consider consumerism as great a threat to capitalism as the ecology movement. By consumerism business seems to mean unreasonable requests, demands, and expectations of consumers with respect to price, quality, ecological considerations, and safety. This indeed is a mixed bag of externalities and market considerations. Ralph Nader is often considered the evil genius associated with the consumer cult.

The ideological bases of consumerism and business differ in that conceptions of limits of technology and of the moralities of production and distribution are not shared. The utopian ideal that more is better than less is shared by business and consumerism. How the more is obtained and for whom is the disagreement. Consumerism and Zero Economic Growth, however, seem to be at opposite ends of the economic spectrum. Z.E.G., at its extreme, appears in recent years to have lost its sting. Consumerism still is a lively issue, and probably will grow livelier in more prosperous times. Business as an institution, unlike consumerism is more interested in production and sales than in the general distribution of the national dividend. Indeed to business distribution means selling. To the economist it means the parcelling of claims to income among the members of society.

Government bureaucrats are generally, in the business perception, unimaginative, dull, and unable to grasp the essential tempo and requirements of business. Politicians are generally viewed as mainly responsive to their desire to be reelected. But one observes that hanging on to a job is not peculiar to politicians. Businessmen, too, have been known to temper their policies and behavior with a desire to stay on the payroll.

To complete the list of those whom business managers consider adversaries one must add the professoriat. In general, again according to Silk and Vogel, professors, glib with words and glittering ideas, often simply do not understand how markets—or capitalism—works. The sociologists are excoriated as the main culprits, although not the only ones. What the businessmen are complaining of, it would seem, is the role and significance of professors in affecting public thinking. But one wonders why single out sociologists?

Academics are a vocal and ink-stained race. Their stock in trade is ideas, some good, some bad. They have a captive audience in their students; they sometimes have access to what in these latter days we call the media. This means that professors write and speak with sufficient interest to claim an audience. Insofar as they concern themselves with public issues, they add the fuel of their ideas and biases to the public debate and discussion. This creates revisions in old conceptions of convention and law. The business community, as one would expect, has fewer people skilled in the area of free-wheeling thinking and public communication. Madison Avenue may sell soap, but it does not distribute ideas. One might suggest that the range of ideas, and hence notions of public and private business behavior, is broader among academics than among businessmen. Hence the academics pose more theoretical considerations than the business community, which is more administrative-minded.

The blanket criticism of professors, as a race, does not ring true in the experience of hundreds of economists, engineers, marketing experts, system analysts, lawyers, geologists, et al. who teach in universities and colleges. Businessmen often hire their expertise, and usually at handsome prices. Furthermore, businessmen sometimes leave the ratrace of business for academic posts, often deanships of business schools.

Businessmen seem satisfied, even pleased, with the training of students who graduate from schools of business. Indeed the M.B.A. and or the M.S.B.A. are degrees which often are keys to the gates of good jobs. The Ph.D., too, is much more common in business than a generation ago. One should also add that posts in government often attract business people. Indeed since the federal salary reforms of the last twenty years, and since Washington found it wise (or expedient) to dilute academic ideas and expertise with business realism and administrative ability, each successive Washington administration has attracted businessmen as well as academics into positions of managerial responsibility.

Why are not more business people in government? Modern business in America rarely creates well known and respected charismatic figures. Business, especially big business, is too technical, and too limiting. A Linowitz of Xerox, or a Blumenthal of Bendix, might consider public service, but many business people usually are not so motivated. If called on, to be sure, they respond. Times of war or other times of great social stress do activate the glands of public service.

As an aside we note that in good times and bad, the agents of business—the high priests of society, the lawyers—are often called on. Lawyers know the omens, the rites, and the laws. They are articulate, flexible, and sharp. The contribution of business to government, from the high level personnel viewpoint, has probably been lawyers. And it has been a noteworthy contribution even if their names rarely become household words like Jaworski's or their deeds front page stories like the exploits of Joseph Welch who brought down Senator Joe McCarthy.

The years since Nixon have been hard on the public image of business, although the Lockheed and Penn Central problems, occurring before Mr. Nixon departed, did not sit well with the press and the sentient public. Business complaints about the irresponsibility of academics, bureaucrats, and consumers, as Silk and Vogel interpret them, cannot be taken very seriously. The complaints are that: government will not listen to the facts of life which are the needs of business; professors (sociologists?) teach contra capitalism; consumers, a minority with Nader as their head, want something called justice, which is not in the cards. These complaints go to the heart of the public conception of morality and ideology. Long before Watergate, the Vietnam War, and the growing inflation and unemployment, a social malaise was noticeable. The Johnson administration was destroyed by it. Nixon's span in office worsened a bad situation. The complaints cited by business seem to be reactions to the many problems of economic society. Mr. Carter's trouble is not only with the oil companies, it is with consumers, even unorganized consumers. But the oil industry is probably even more vulnerable than Mr. Carter to consumer wrath. Consumers ultimately control the Congress. It is as if the rabble, outside the mystery of business, but the ultimate political masters, and penultimately an unreasoning giant unschooled in the decorum of business, which frightens business. The professors may be seen as those who articulate the inarticulate demands of the rabble.

In the spirit of Silk and Vogel's report we may liken politicians, consumers, and professors to the rabble. It tends to expect more from the business system than they are likely to get because business simply has not the ability to produce what is expected, and because of the very structure of the social world.

Business is market-oriented. It tries to satisfy the market and to build up demand (market). To expect business to manage the whole complex economic world is not only wrong from the viewpoint of the business function, it is nonsensical on social grounds. Business is not government.

Business considers itself preeminent in the social setting, because after all, without production, and production at the high levels the nation enjoys, well-being, art, culture, and politics would be impossible or at least impoverished.

Business spokesmen (according to Silk and Vogel), or at least some of them who consider this aspect of society, tend to see themselves as operating in two systems—political democracy and the market (capitalist) system. The one acting as if it were the more powerful and demanding is the political. The fall guy is the market. Such a dichotomy of interest has no easily available mechanism for adjust-ment.[5] In such a system decisions, if they can be called decisions, are *not* the adjustment of the interaction of equals. By all odds govern-ment is the more powerful.

That business sees itself weaker than or inferior to government is a point of view we do not find disturbing.[6] We omit the technical aspects of government regulation, which to the knowledgeable observer, sometimes appear inept and ill conceived. We leave out the administra-tive aspects, so often pettifogging. We look only to the moral aspects. Government is the spokesman for the common will. To be sure the spokesman sometimes misspeaks, sometimes confuses superficial values with deeper ideology, but nevertheless it is government which is the necessary means to the degree of social harmony a nation must have to be viable.

4

THE DEATH OF DIOGENES

Diogenes, it is reported, went about ancient Athens searching, in daylight, with a lantern trying to find an honest man. I suspect that if he were to try to do the same thing today in many modern cities, he would be mugged, the lantern ripped off, his robe stripped off, the culprits looking for a few bucks; after which he would be arrested, booked, and tossed into the slammer for creating a public disturbance.

Yet this does not mean that the ancient did not or modern world does not know right from wrong. Diogenes today would in all likelihood find that in many places he would be ignored or possibly treated as an interesting promotional gimmick. He might even be featured in the evening news as a human interest item and ultimately become a guest on a talk show. Even if he were received in a kindly way, Diogenes would have some trouble finding his object, not because there are no honest men but because the criteria of right and wrong, honest and dishonest, have become considerably more confusing than they were even in so complex a society as Athens.

The idea of management is complex. The words "to manage," "manager," and "management" have to do with the conduct of an operation which is controllable, and whose alternative possible outcomes may differ as to acceptability. One does not manage an earthquake. The study of earthquakes is of great practical importance, for we *might* learn how to manage one. Management in this sense is complex for a multitude of alternatives intrude themselves.[1]

A chemical reaction is neither good nor bad. But if there are alternative ways of getting the reaction, we do label some ways better than others. Criteria are mensurate; the relative effectiveness of one type of procedure rather than another in reaction time, pollution generated, money costs, and so on, determines the economy of producing the chemical reaction. The choices of procedure and technique are in the control of the scientist. He, in our conception, is a manager. The notions of good or bad, in a basic operational sense implied here, are akin to efficiency or effectiveness. Morality and ethics are not involved.

The study of marketing is important, for it teaches how to manage, i.e., to behave economically, in the market. We differentiate good from bad management in the light of what the manager gets out of the operation, or how well he controls it. Managing is also evaluated by the economy of the inputs it requires. Results and inputs are valuable and costly. Costs and returns may not always be easily measured in terms of money, but ultimately they can be reduced at least to opportunity or alternative costs and returns. Something costs what is given up to get it. Wherever alternatives of cost and return are involved, an economy of some sort is implied. We are accustomed to thinking in terms of money measures and criteria, and for a market economy such custom is appropriate.[2]

But we also think in terms of the economy of verbal expression or of lines in drawings. A good Picasso line drawing may evoke a myriad of ideas and memories in the observer. Yet the drawing may consist of only half a dozen lines superbly juxtaposed and firmly sketched. Similarly a St. John could write, "In the beginning was the Word, and the Word was with God, and the Word was God." Regardless of one's theological or cosmological beliefs, the sentence does express clearly and succinctly a mystical metaphysic which might be elaborated into a book of mystical theology. Economy means using the fewest inputs to get a desired output.

The easiest economy to measure, we suppose, is the market economy.[3] Money costs can be counted by any number of people skilled in the accounting of costs and returns, and the answers will be approximately the same or subject to discussion within a defined framework of concepts. The discussion of alternative accounting techniques is a rational one. Similarly income generated can be accounted for by those skilled in the art of accounting. Differences as to the role of inventories and their evaluation, or the nature and function of accruals or even risk, can be reasonably discussed if there are differences of opinion. Again ethics and morality are not involved until the accounting procedures are considered in the light of acceptable or legally determined behavior.

But the easiest part (although it is hard enough) of business is the accounting for costs and returns and related measures. The harder parts are putting together or changing the operation of the enterprise, making decisions as to what the inputs should be, and what the outputs are likely to be. Among the inputs and outputs of course, are considerations of legal right and wrong. Such decisions and operational controls are the stuff of management. Not the least of the managerial functions is bearing the responsibility for the decisions, which in reality are often, perhaps usually, in a large firm, made by agents or surrogates for the management.

An electrician is to be hired or fired. If the company employs 500 or 50,000, this act is not important to the firm. But it is important to the electrician and his family, to the members of his crew, and possibly to the specific function the electrician performs in the firm. The manager has no knowledge of the electrician's fate, except via the impersonal manual of employment, as it is known to the front office. The odds are that the front office has only the vaguest notion of what goes on in Personnel with regard to the hiring and/or firing of electricians.

But delegation does not dissolve responsibility. Someone in the firm has made a decision which affects the firm, and management (read "The Manager") is ultimately involved and responsible. Perhaps this explains why otherwise clever and bright managers are so often unwilling (or psychologically unable) to delegate authority within the span of their easily recognized responsibilities. If they are to be held responsible, then they will have their say. Yet we never heard of a manager of a large firm who typed his own letters. He may check on his letters personally. We have, however, known high officials to *handwrite* extremely important communications, for secrecy as well as to indicate to the reader their utter involvement in the item being considered. Responsibility, like economy, is clearly a characteristic of management.

There is a third element, in addition to economizing and bearing responsibility, which may not be so obvious or so easy to grasp. The third element is ethics. "Be upright and walk with God" is poetry and not an operational procedure. So by ethical behavior we do not mean obedience to some aphorism, or obedience to an inner voice which all of us are reputed to have but which is often stilled or not listened to. Conscience may make cowards of us all, but the conscience of each of us is unique, or so we enjoy believing. Conscience itself is the product of our times and experiences, possibly our genes, and is multifaceted and supremely fickle. That some persons can be bought, perhaps that all can, is not a gold star for the integrity of conscience. Institutions are ways of general behavior; it is the individual who is the actor, in the final analysis. The effects of action, too, are on individuals. Social actions, which come down to personal acts, to persist and be acceptable, must be (socially) legitimated. From this view, conscience is socially defined. It is a set of learned values which, when converted to behavior, are judged by the ideological values of time, place, and circumstances.

When slavery no longer could be socially (not economically or legally) justified, the institution was abolished. The immediate effects were on former slaves and former owners. But ultimately the whole society, the whole world, were involved. Indeed the late twentieth century surely would be different if American slavery had not occurred or had been abolished in a fashion different from the way it had.

When the legitimacy of certain drugs, e.g., saccharine, marijuana or laetrile, is questioned, arguments of science, law, private and public morality, and public opinion (sometimes confused with advertising) are all brought to bear on the issues and so, ultimately, on the concerned individuals. A lady from Philadelphia tells the world via television that her diabetic son is entitled to a sweet taste; and the risk of kidney cancer twenty years from now is less significant than sweetness now. She wants saccharine. The surgeon general's office, estimating the data, disagrees. Which argument will ultimately prevail as an expression of social ethic? Conscience, public or private, becomes a resultant of current and historical forces, and may even be different for different people. Some Catholics are unnerved by the Mass being sung in a modern language, while Protestants and Jews are notorious for having created a host of alternative churches to communicate with and receive directions from the Host.

So ethics is not a simple, unique entity which all who seek may find. Yet ethical considerations are part of the ultimate legitimation for social behavior. To do something because it is morally right is generally viewed as a better justification merely because it is expedient. Yet the expedient may also be morally right. It all depends on the analysis. Appropriate economic and responsible behavior also depend on analysis and point of view. In the affairs of business, economic behavior has somehow to conform to legitimated behavior. It is the economic which, in a moral world, has to adjust. But ideology, for its part, has to conform to the exigencies of reality. Law and convention are pliable in the light of the requirements of income generation, employment, and price levels. It is because business is so intimately connected with the national welfare that managers, as business leaders and spokesmen, have a status and authority generally above other social groups. Even government has to give special consideration to business need, if such need can be defined and persuasively stated.

Managers like other people want to be significant. They hope for a moral worth high in their own eyes and in the eyes of the beholders.[4] The need for moral acceptability, we can state without much fear of contradiction, is an axiom for most people. Few people willingly choose a wrong or bad action with a legitimating rationalization. One can imagine perpetrators of what is generally seen as evil justifying their behavior by a morality which goes beyond conventional good and evil. The insecurity of our conceptions of good and evil probably accounts for the fascination so many quite law-abiding people feel for Nietzsche, the Mafia, and other critics of "bourgeois ethics." But very few want to serve evil, unless conventional evil is transvalued into some sort of a good beyond the comprehension of unimaginative people. Devil worshippers, followers of arcane deities moral revolutionaries who would revise values, have different conceptions of good and bad from the rest of us. The self-anointed hero imagines a good beyond (ordinary) good and evil. The truly dissolute, those who are not concerned with the evil consequences of their actions, are probably very rare.

Moral criticism is usually of three sorts: (1) the complaint that the values of the ideology are in disarray because they are not observed; (2) the complaint that the values of the ideology are really immoral and so a transvaluation of values is required; or (3) the assertion that the values of ideology do not apply to the business at hand.

Among the great mass of people in America, as well as among businessmen, there is only a vague agreement as to what good and bad are in the abstract, or in the concrete. Usually fairly general agreements can be reached on specific actions; or at the opposite end of the moral spectrum, on very vague, general, nonoperational principles. Murder, forgery, and arson are usually among the disallowed, while honesty, love of country, and possibly the reliance on the free enterprise system are among the positive elements, the last for most of the business community.

Murder, arson, and forgery are criminal concepts, embodied in law. They have little or nothing to do with commercial ethics, while honesty, a positive notion, is difficult to define in many business situations. Is honesty served by consumer advertising? Who has ever enjoyed the mileage per gallon of gasoline which Detroit, abetted by Madison Avenue, half promises? Will a certain shaving lotion assure a sailor a knockout beauty in every (or any) port? Are Exxon, Dupont, and US Steel, to name only three firms, really so consumer and science-oriented as they claim, or is their first loyalty to their firms, broadly viewed?

Only naive consumers, and others affected by the self-proclaimed virtues of business, concern themselves with the content of the ads. Most people, one hopes, are amused or dismayed (or should be) by the cleverness or dullness of the advertisement. The consumer hopes that the claims made by the advertiser for his product are approximately true, and that the contents of the product are fairly stated. In point of fact, aspirin does relieve headaches. But does Compoze cause complications as the Food and Drug Administration claims? Did the manufacturer know of the alleged effects while selling the product with the contents fairly stated but clearly beyond the understanding of the typical user?

How much information, analysis, reports of testing are required to make an ad honest? If the law requires certain standards, and they are complied with, is the firm honest or merely law-abiding? The two concepts, ethical and legal, are not the same. Compliance with the law is a *legal* necessity, and has nothing to do with honesty in the abstract.[5]

Yet not all laws and conventions are obeyed to the letter, some are not at all, and unethical actions may be committed by people we should consider honest. This is true in our private lives as well as in our business activity, even where the law is certain. White lies and skilled disobedience to some laws are part of the art of living.

The U.S. Supreme Court (1977) held that an employee whose religion required abstinence from gainful employment on Saturday was not legally assured of his job. A holy Saturday off was not required of management if the cost and trouble of managing seniority list schedules, possible overtime payments, etc., were too great, in the opinion of the employer. In other words, the right to exercise one's religion is not an absolute right but must be considered in the light of the rights (constitutional and otherwise) of *all* persons affected.

Now prior to the decision there was a great deal of uncertainty about the legal and constitutional protection of religious observance. Conceding that the instant decision has not nailed down the religious rights problem in industry, it is clear that prior to June 14, 1977, the several interested lawyers and personnel administrators were not in agreement on the question. Certainty in law is a sometime thing.

But for many, probably most, issues which face the business decision maker one may assume a high degree of certainty as to what the law means. The courts, in fact, only deal with the tiniest fraction of the legal decisions made by business managers. But not *all* business decisions need be in strict accordance with legal requirements. The value of the issue in doubt to the parties involved must be worth more than the costs, toil, and trouble to adjudicate the matter, before one considers calling in the lawyers and judges. The cost of adjudication is often so high as to effectively block recourse to the law to determine what is or is not legal behavior.

The fact that legislatures delegate authority over detail to administrative agencies, e.g., state liquor authorities or the Federal Communications Commission, leads some business people to question, by complaint to the administrative agency or to the courts, the rules and administrative regulations of such bodies. Honest differences as to the intent of state legislatures or the federal Congress may motivate such complaints, the very content of the regulations being questioned. But in more cases than can be counted, administrative regulations or provisions of law are not considered sufficiently significant to justify bringing legal action.

Nor do administrators and police enforce all the laws and regulations extant. Were all the traffic and vehicle rules to be insistently obeyed, traffic in big cities would be different from what it is, probably more chaotic. Were all the provisions of the building codes adhered to scrupulously, single dwelling construction would become more costly than many people could afford, and so on.

The point is that there is a kind of unwritten agreement or social convention as to which aspects of laws and rules will be enforced or followed, and under what circumstances other aspects may be neglected. At what value does a Christmas gift become a bribe to a purchasing agent? and how does one distinguish between a friendly gesture to and pressure on a government agent? When the author, many years ago, was in a group of government officials investigating the fishing industry, the field visits alternated between visits to cold and unpleasant fish piers and processing plants to plush trips on fishing vessels, probably especially cleaned up, with meals of extraordinary quality, taste, and service. Were the plush accommodations a bribe or merely a polite gesture?

Where the social conventions are violated, or the intent is clear, then of course what was offered ostensibly as a polite gesture becomes what was intended, an improper pressure on a public official, a minor bribe. The former dean of a famous veterinary college once admitted that, unless 10 percent of the places in his school were reserved for students who entered by pressure from politicians, the budget of the school which the legislature voted would have been so curtailed that the school would have been in deep trouble. Bribery of such a sort becomes a convention. The unadmitted students are the injured parties.

It is obviously easier to fix a traffic ticket than a murder rap; or to arrange for a small modification to a single dwelling in a lower income neighborhood than to get away with polluting a stream. The house change is an extralegal variance which often is winked at, provided it is minor. It may often be accomplished by a contractor or homeowner who simply does the work, getting no formal approval. After all, City Hall is not likely to force a homeowner to tear out $500 worth of back porch, which offends no one, simply because it extends a foot beyond the building's foundation. Pollution, however, is a different problem. The public and press are currently pollution-conscious. People and animals do get sick from foul water. Streams run into rivers, and so in comes the federal government; and pollution may keep out federal money.

The significance of the violation is of importance, and the significance may not be the same at different times. In the 1960s when employment was high and jobs easily available, the public concern with ecological matters became almost a national phobia. However by the middle 1970s, with unemployment high, and the economic future uncertain, jobs became more significant than a little pollution. Congress set back automobile emission standards, and coal became an ideal substitute for oil or gas. We may theorize that the true-blue proponents of "saving the environment" often were a minority of young middle-class college students for whom the harsh realities of earning a living had not yet been internalized, or persons whose attention to the environment was obsessive.

The kind of conventional and adaptive behavior discussed above may be viewed as a thick or thin protective covering against the cutting edge of the sword of the law. More significant to the manager, however, are the conventions of business, the market, and trade which have no particular connection with legislation. They may be trade association canons of conduct or simply habits of behavior and ways of doing things which have grown up in an industry or market. The determination of who gets keys to the executive toilets, or allowing employees to use company cars for private purposes are examples of custom or convention. The examples are really minor conventions, and are more concerned with personal benefits than with questions of ideology and morality.

Industry, in its public concern at least, focuses on consumer relations as the major ethical issue. Presumably market arrangements are viewed as legally and judicially determined. Self-interest is hedged by law and the courts, and the game is won or at least points are scored if ingenuity can accomplish in some way what previous actions could not because of the legal and market limitations. Such procedures are not to be criticized. They have nothing to do with ethics, but rather with respect for law and reliance on the convention of competition.

The major social implications of business morality are in the creation of business conventions, and in the generation of laws governing business behavior. For while adherence to law and convention may be morally neutral and expected, the conventions and laws themselves are judged and legitimated against the ideological bundle of values in action.[6]

Government and nongovernment institutions are often—one might say usually—sensitive to business needs as explained or asserted by business spokesmen. Employment, prices, output, the most significant elements in the nation's standard of living and welfare, are involved. It is almost comic to hear an employee (even an unemployed ex-employee) or a labor leader explain why a business firm, or business in general, had to engage in actions which clearly were against the interests of labor or consumers. The Steel Workers Union helped the industry get protection against the imports of Japanese steel in 1977-78 to the detriment of consumers and of labor in steel-using industries. The unions adversely affected did not publicly object. In the bitter winter strike of the coal miners in the same year, public opinion and the opinion of many non-coal mine workers were against the strike, i.e., against the United Mine Workers and for the industry. (Even President Miller of the UMW was ambivalent.) In a similar vein, in the anti-trust suit against the Atlantic and Pacific grocery chain, competitors took ads in newspapers castigating the government, presumably for trying to prohibit improper market actions by A & P which hurt the protesters.

Without attempting any evaluation of such attitudes, we can see that business, as an institution, differs from most other institutions in the governmental and social concern it engenders, especially when there is a threat to the livelihood of many, or to the welfare of the republic. It is of more than passing interest that in such circumstances few intellectuals, e.g., economists, politicians, newspaper and magazine writers, editors, and educators, seek alternative ways of organizing markets and allocating resources. Manipulation or management of markets is considered less frequently than the interventions into markets to get some desired results.

Yet some interventions, like restricting steel imports below a given price, or further complicating an already complicated health insurance system in the coal industry, are, in the opinion of virtually no knowledgeable person, likely to work. By 1978 the 1977 "reforms" in the Social Security system secured by raising the tax rates were under dire public and congressional criticism, actually *before* the new rates became effective.

Business has a special place in governmental and social policy consideration. To maintain the general ideological system and social system, with its market orientation and business appendage, the business managers should, as a matter of institutional preservation, ask for laws and negotiate conventional behavior which are in accord with the deep-seated tenets of justice and morality of the society, or, on the other hand, adopt ameliorative practices to make corrective law unnecessary. Since the interests of business are not of a simple piece, but rather often peculiar to particular firms, regions, and industries, compromise, generosity, and common sense are required if the outcomes are to be good—that is, moral and operational. It is this kind of policy making which probably will determine the future of the business institution and its morality. The role of the intellectuals, those who articulate legitimation or its lack, and those who suggest alternative procedures of social and economic behavior, cannot be overestimated.

At the consumer level however public opinion, i.e., consumer acceptance, is a consideration which is not necessarily or even mainly determined by law. Consumers may like or dislike the way they are treated by the seller. They may feel the product is worth the price or not. Advertising, consumer relations, quality, price, services, all play roles in achieving consumer acceptance. Since law and convention are usually not major issues when consumers reject or accept a product, the ingenuity of the seller is given a free rein. One of the constant concerns of sellers who deal directly with consumers is that the relationship be smooth and agreeable. Since many products, at the consumer level, are sold through retailers who are not closely tied to any manufacturer, or through large manufacturer-controlled selling organizations such as Avon Products, manufacturers are often desirous of developing conventional behavior which is appealing to consumers.

Large organizations and uncontrolled retailers have to be controlled lest they fail to maintain consumer confidence. To this end rules of conduct or codes of ethics are established. Firms or trade associations may develop such rules, treating them as conventions of appropriate behavior.

Arch N. Booth,[7] a former president of the U.S. Chamber of Commerce, in discussing such codes feels that businessmen are full of "concern and good intentions" toward their buyers. Working through trade associations, business accomplishes its good intentions by valiantly setting up restraints and procedures for correcting flaws in the consumer relation. Self-regulation rather than implied (i.e., legislated) rule is the ideal. The argument seems to mean that industry must take "voluntary action" lest legislation be imposed; for unless voluntarism in honesty and ethics occurs, "coercive regulation" and "centralized authority" will suppress freedom. The argument is not a clear call for ethical business behavior. It rather is an argument for avoiding government regulation. It is difficult to see the connection between being just and moral as a principle and following a course of action because the alternative is costly. The good and just results may follow from prudent action, but the motive is not ethical, it is self-protective. Convention is relied on to accomplish self-interest.

The Direct Selling Association, according to Neil Offen[8] its senior vice president and legal counsel, accounts for about 50 percent of total industry sales. Of the several thousand direct selling firms in the United States, only a "hundred or so" are in the D.S.A. Under their procedures a consumer who feels aggrieved makes a complaint in writing, and five steps are then undertaken to examine the issue and come to a decision. ("Justice delayed is justice denied" seems a forgotten adage.) The trade association, in effect, polices the actions of its members. "Peer group pressure" and the threat of public embarrassment are the techniques of keeping members honest. Mr. Offen believes the public does not know about the program, that it is not used as fully as it might be. The time and trouble for a consumer to take the five steps necessary to right the wrong of a transaction worth only a few dollars is probably excessive for most consumers who buy door to door products. The other function of D.S.A. is to lobby against legislation which might be restrictive. In advising members to draw up uniform codes, it is urged that such codes be legally defensible.

Other codes of ethics are discussed by various authors in *The Ethical Basis of Economic Freedom,*[9] which is a kind of standard explanation of business ethics by business leaders. It appears that the canons of the legal profession do not suggest that lawyers seek justice, but rather that they act "zealously" to improve the legal system although the oath of admission as promulgated by the American Bar Association requires an attorney not to engage in a suit or proceeding which appears to the attorney to be unjust, except when it is believed that the issue is debatable under the law.

What is unnerving about the essays is that the authors, all representatives of trade associations, are less concerned with the morality of the behavior of the retailers they are speaking for as measured by public acceptance or ideology than with creating an arbitrary ideology and assuming it is moral!

But physicians, in fact, are openly criticized for their Medicare and Medicaid practices and for their fees. Real estate dealers are not a beloved class among private home buyers and sellers. Television programs are not only a wasteland but they are a jungle of vulgarity and violence. Collegiate football has been suspect for as long as one can remember. Yet the commentators all assume the respectives codes and ethical endeavors are the basis for justice and morality. One weakness is that such codes are unilaterally issued. The parties affected consumers—have no voice in their preparation. Legislation, resulting from social pulls and tugs in its preparation, would probably be more equitable than rules of behavior prepared by an interest group mainly in their own interest. The adage "It takes two to tango" is more appropriate, in these cases, than "God helps those who help themselves."

And so Diogenes of Ancient Greece, were he to come alive in modern America would have a complex job to sort out the honest business people from the less honest. The criteria which made sense in the Old World would not fit the actions of the New. The ethical principles of the two societies undoubtedly have much in common, but the details would be literally worlds apart.

5

ISN'T CITY HALL ON OUR TURF?

"You can't fight City Hall" is an American aphorism which, from
time to time, is proved wrong. California's Proposition 13 backed
political officeholders into a corner. Even beyond the borders of the
Golden State, politicians reacted to the voter threat. Proposition 13
and its imitations are not likely to make up much of the substance
of American economic policy in the long run. The Proposition, did,
however, make changes in the way governments behave more likely.
City Hall took note.

This discussion is an observation on the desirability of policy goals
being explicit. If they are explicit, business managers may have a voice
in their creation, along with other groups in society. Compromise on
goals is a democratic way, or at least a reasonable way. However the
choice of goals is related to the means of attaining them, and to their
interconnections with other issues. To ride a cock horse to Banbury
Cross is possible only if horses are available, and making horses available takes more than a small effort.

Philosophers, or at least some philosophers, are strange, even scary
people. Some have to prove they exist, others are not sure the world
exists; while still others argue that being and becoming—that is,
existence—is a sometime thing. On the whole, we think the last
group have made an interesting case.

We suggest that the phrase "being and becoming" be transposed,
for in order that something "be" it must have first "become." In

other words, reality is structured out of our knowledge, or sensations of reality. In this sense, reality as a specific—business ethics—is what we are investigating, and it is constructed out of our impressions and analysis of behavior. All this sounds far out, but it really is important in understanding how business people grasp and evaluate their own behavior and the behavior of others.

How can we structure the reality of motives and morality for a firm or a society? These are complex institutions, guided and motivated by a host of forces. To be sure, we cannot know all, or perhaps even the major, forces which motivate people's choosing one or another goal. We can however, speculate about the overt or covert nature ascribed to motives and goals.

The view of many economists, and of others who believe the world moves inexorably to an equilibrium, is that the ultimate goal (equilibrium) is implicit in the system. Thus we have the famous aphorism of traditional economists and even many businessmen and politicians, "Laissez faire-laissez passer." Let well enough alone. If you interfere, you will only make things worse. This is a free translation, because proponents of laissez faire urge that interference by government in the economic or social order generates a less good society, except that certain social functions, such as the police function, are a necessary intervention. The view in the fine phrase of the Spanish philosopher Ortega y Gasset is that "order is not pressure which is imposed on society from without, but an equilibrium which is set up from within." In this view, the purpose, the goal of social endeavor is *implicit* in the very mechanism of the endeavor.

It is a comforting philosophy, and not always a bad one. Anyone who as a child has tried to repair or even take apart a pocket watch knows how complex and frustrating the mechanism is. Trying to fix it, which usually presupposes a physical analysis, usually ends up in total destruction. If a watch is complex and frustrating in its design and operation, how much more complex and frustrating must a poverty program or price-wage control be!

The response of those who hold to explicit goal setting is obvious. A child does not know how to fix a watch, but a watchmaker does. Take the timepiece to an expert, and he will do the job properly. If you want to construct a poverty program go to an expert. But, respond the implicit protagonists, "Where are the experts in poverty programs or wage-price controls to stop inflation? All past efforts have been failures. And furthermore inflation usually is ended by forces quite unrelated to conscious price-wage regulation." It is usually held that the preparation for World War 2 ended the Great Depression and not Mr. Roosevelt's political medicine! The argument is indeterminate and unsatisfying. We therefore enter the fray, armed with analysis but not assured of answers and outcome.

With respect to the implicit good and goodness of a laissez faire system, however, analysis may be irrelevant. We are not mainly concerned with a theoretical system or model. One cannot "plug" justice or morality into a model and get very meaningful results. As we have indicated, different situations call forth or rely on different ideological forces and legitimations. In the real world—or perhaps we should say in the real worlds, for conceptions of reality differ, as we have suggested—in the real worlds short term problems often require social action before considerations of justice or morality are adequately addressed. Such action is usually not mainly economic in its nature. That is, allocation of resources, relative prices, and savings and investments are less stressed than welfare issues. Poor people, for example, have become relatively poorer as compared to the average of the society; or some ethnic or otherwise defined groups are having a hard time, or raising unshirted hell with the political or social organization. A 40 percent unemployment rate among black and Hispanic young people in New York, Chicago, or Los Angeles transcends economic issues. Pollution, urban disintegration, support of the arts, national defense, and a hundred other problems may require economic and business resources, but they are not essentially economic or business problems.

The question is, "Can the government intervene in legitimate social problems, without exacerbating the problems, or creating more onerous ones by reallocating resources?" The answer is, "We do not know for sure, but have the feeling that sometimes it can and sometimes it can't."[1]

The failures of government to solve social problems are well known. Inflation, poverty, health, etc., have not responded well to government efforts. Indeed the efforts of OSHA (Occupation Safety and Health Administration) nearly led to a political explosion until President Carter instructed Secretary of Labor Marshall to change the rules and methods of enforcement. Few would argue that the efforts to integrate urban schools have improved the public school system; once the center jewel in the American crown.

But on the other hand public health efforts have virtually eradicated many diseases and sharply reduced, perhaps to zero, the terrible threats of epidemic. Technical education flourishes, and with it science and technology. The poor are better cared for than in the distant past. Bucketshops no longer cheat small investors in the stock market, at least not so obviously as they did before Mr. Roosevelt's Securities and Exchange Commission. And the list can be lengthened.

But we have paid a social price for intervention. Part of the price is failure of some of the interventions; part is a reduction in the freedoms business had prior to the intervention; and part is losses to consumers because of the unwillingness or inability of business to enter certain fields of endeavor.

1. *Failure of intervention.*[2] The cost to taxpayers and consumers of the various programs of the past ten or fifteen years to help the poor are staggering, even if the sum has not been calculated. Not only have many programs simply failed, such as attempts to set up "corps" to teach and train youth in big cities, or CETA (Comprehensive Education and Training Administration), but, more significantly, the failures took the place of other possible programs which might have been established and might have been more successful. These were lost, often permanently, because the programs constituted were half baked and poorly administered. Each failure caused many to doubt the capacity of government to do anything well. The crisis in government of the late twentieth century is the popular loss of faith in government's capacity to do a job, any job, well.

The CETA program of 1977–78 was a subsidy program to train and educate the unemployed in public jobs which would enable them to enter the labor market in the private or public sectors in a more usual way. The cities, states, and other public agencies involved, however, tended more often than not to treat CETA funds as part of their regular budget. People were often hired not as "trainees" but as employees. Boondoggles, too, became part of the effort. When the end of the first fiscal period arrived and no more money was available, confusion and recrimination reigned. The criticism from both (subsidized) employees and the local (subsidized) governments was that CETA had somehow created an obligation for the federal government to maintain the jobs and keep the money flowing.

But the Proposition 13 revolt of California had so frightened politicians that more money was simply out of the question. Not only was the CETA program itself largely a failure, but it had caused hope to flourish that more was to come. The program was negative in its immediate impact and destructive in its implication. It will be harder to try to solve the same problem next time round. If taxes are not used effectively the society suffers. The disposable income of taxpayers is reduced by the taxes paid. The hopes of those for whom the taxes were to provide useful programs are dashed. The prestige of government is reduced. And the reallocation of the nation's resources by the payments to the failed program, directly or indirectly affect all other markets.

2. *Loss of Business Freedom:* This is a difficult issue because in some areas of activity intervention is properly considered beyond reproach. For example, in the early 1900s the workman's compensation movement was attacked by some in the business community as being an unwarranted interference by government in the employer-employee relation. But the need for direct intervention by having the state become the insurer or by allowing a private carrier to insure, was clear ultimately to all the state legislatures. At any rate, workman's compensation was gradually enacted in all the states, and has been, as an institution, a success.[3] No one seriously wants to abolish it, although experts do not consider the laws and their administration perfect. Business freedom to contract with employees was restrained, but no one was hurt. When social security and unemployment compensation were first considered on a national level in the F.D.R. administration, there were complaints and cries of alarm, but the enactment of the Social Security Act has met with general approval, although again the administration and financing are considered improper and even insane by various segments of the society. Yet few, indeed, would want the concepts of social security and unemployment compensation erased from the roster of government intervention. Changed and reformed—yes; abolished—no.

Some kinds of government intervention have been legitimated theoretically, or by experience in the American public opinion. The same cannot be said of other exercises in intervention. The regulation by the Interstate Commerce Commission of railroads and over-the-road hauling has been a hindrance in the minds of many in the railroad and trucking industries, especially to the growth of firms in those industries. Many users find the ICC a hindrance, not a help. Restraints on business growth, permission for rate fixing in the trucking business, and limitations on joint truck-railroad haulage have been frustrating to the less orthodox and probably the more imaginative and less risk-averse firms, and to many users. The attempts of former Chairman Alfred Kahn of the Civil Aeronautics Board to introduce competition into the air carrier industry has frightened some firms, but enlivened the courage to compete in others. The federal restraint on commercial banks paying interest on checking accounts has not given a free hand to banks which would like to use such interest payments as a vehicle of expansion. Examples could be multiplied. What they suggest is that government intervention may, in some instances, discourage business development and support entrenched interests.

Perhaps the greatest intervention by the government is the federal restrictions on size and market practices contained in the anti-trust laws. The issue is of such importance that the ethical and social implications of such restraints deserve a long analysis. At this point, however, let it suffice to point out that the anti-trust policy of the United States is in part based on a laissez faire conception and in part on an explicit goal perception called in the economic jargon "performance criteria."

No one seriously criticizes the government's requiring certain standards of market behavior. "Conspiracy" is not a nice word in any ethical context. It is when the very structure of industry is considered, and the effects of that structure on output, prices, growth, technological improvement, consumers, and competitors, that the issues heat up.

Again conservative, well situated firms tend to like the protection of the status quo, especially if here and there a merger can be profitably consummated. But growth firms and those itching to merge and conglomerate often have gripes at government policies and court decisions. To be sure, the public arguments about consumer protection and similar public spirited assertions, while possibly true, are probably of lower significance to the firm than the goals which the managers have set for themselves and their enterprises as achievable, desirable, and profitable.

3. *The Consumer's Plight.* Insofar as industry is stifled in its growth and performance, consumers are hurt. Prices are probably higher and quantities are less than they might have been. Quality, too, may be adversely affected. But if industry were untrammelled we might have a regime of monopolies or cooperating oligopolies. And then would consumers be worse off? No one can say, in the abstract, what would happen. The issues are *particular* and beg for *particular* analysis. Policy based on particulars is difficult, and not, generally speaking, part of the government's ideology or practice. Government intervention into the behavior and structure of markets is fraught with danger, for the intervention cannot usually be tested by experiment. Social experiments may sometimes be a little like experimenting with suicide. A successful experiment cannot be repeated. One has to rely on mental experiments, which is to say logical analysis and history.

Analysis tends to be abstract; "general theory" is the term often used. This is to say that theoretical analysis tends to abstract out of what is being analyzed the unique or peculiar elements, and to deal with the remaining elements in some ordered, logical fashion. Firms are, in a sense, disembodied in theory and separated from any particular management or setting. These particulars are to be added when the "application" is made, which is to say when the theorist is no longer involved.

In our opinion public or private (firm) economic and business policy suffers if it is very abstract, for what is important to theory may well be trivial to policy. The essence of policy and program is that it is to be applied in changing situations. The realities of personality, given situations, and nonlogical reactions, are essential in understanding particular details and are often significant. Thus policy like any other activity requires not only abstraction (analysis), but memory, imagination, and a knowledge of the particular setting. What is significant in analysis may be less significant in application—that is, policy and program.

There is no clear a priori reason to believe that, given the state of the United States steel industry, it might not be more socially effective to have fewer firms, especially given the competition of nonsteel products. Nor is there reason to believe that the public utility policy of the United States is generally favorable to consumers. The nuclear energy problem with the dangers of waste and accident suggests issues which go beyond the mere economic. Do the deep sea fishing restraints hurt or help consumers? Should the Big Three in automobiles be allowed to own, or even have a large control in, distribution? These are questions which economic theory cannot answer; these are particular policy questions. The issues involved are difficult not only to analyze but even to define.

At all three levels of consideration—the political, the industrial, and the consumer—public policy, which is to say ideology and thus public morality and ethics, is involved quite explicitly. But we must conclude from this discussion that, in a world so interrelated and complex, to rely for guidance on a laissez faire, implicit goal and ethic is to be unrealistically abstract, or perhaps even theological. Explicit goal setting (in business called "management by objective") is not only desirable, it is necessary. But explicit goal setting involves dealing with interrelations, interconnections, and conflicting interests which can easily become overwhelming.

In a sense, society is damned if it does follow explicit goals and damned if it doesn't. Is there a solution?[4]

Fortunately there is a partial solution. In a word, it is "restraint." And the restraint should be conditioned by the analysis of the problem and the policy goals sought.

Not every issue which is raised in government by interested parties regarding alleged business failures or social frictions requires public action, especially when the action can be only of a palliative nature. Business or minor governmental distress, if not general, does not necessarily require an act of Congress. Government is not the only institution with responsibility.

Let us freely grant that some business practices are antisocial by generally acceptable standards—for example, price fixing. The ancient laws on conspiring and collusion have recognized this as an evil for nearly a thousand years. Whenever and wherever it appears, it should be attacked. Except of course where the government itself is the price fixer. Here is where the restraint comes in. Price fixing by government for regulated industries is a delicate, sensitive task. Those most likely to be hurt are the buyers of the commodities or services whose prices are being fixed, and the labor employed. Investors in price-fixed industries are not exempt from some of the risks of investment, as is reflected in the dividends or interest they expect and receive. But the consumers are always vulnerable, as well as the suppliers of alternative goods and services. In brief, we are suggesting that government price regulation of, say, a public utility requires a sophisticated analysis and program of action which should be evaluated by disinterested experts, not for its moral content but for its analytic soundness. The moral content will be evaluated by the legislature and by all who are affected.

The same type of consideration should apply to anti-trust legislation and policy, and to all other interventions. The government then would be forced to temper its behavior to the critical evaluation of experts. The government would also be forced to state, overtly, its goals so that public opinion would be able to legitimate or refuse legitimation. Legitimation would not be buried in means so as to make the ends appear as necessary. A neat organizational chart, or an efficient organization, does not assure that the end products are desirable.

Similar safeguards for explication of goals and means might apply to other kinds of intervention which are not so openly economic in their nature. A second opinion and the articulation of hoped-for goals are not unreasonable prior conditions.

Business, which is to say management, too would have the opportunity to state its case, as it has presently. But the analysis, openly offered, would permit management to exercise both a critical comment and an adjustive stance or procedure before the constraint were applied.

The hearing which the Congress and other legislative bodies hold on legislation partly performs the function of examining the implications of proposed legislation. The House of Representatives relies for budget making on a special in-House agency responsible to it. House and Senate committees have staff advice which is often imaginative and technically skilled. The president, too, relies on advice of experts invited to White House conferences, and on the technical staffs of the various administrative agencies. But such advisory bodies, which should be continued and strengthened, tend to have at least two weaknesses.

First, they are, generally speaking, committed to a point of view, a policy, and a program. They are hired to give advice to their employers. Second, the tendency is, even in the Bureau of Management and Budget, to treat issues as fairly isolated.

The monetary crisis and the energy crisis of the 1970s illustrate the latter criticism. The two crises are obviously related in a number of ways, through foreign exchange and balance of payment questions and through domestic costs and prices. Such connections have been acknowledged.

However the legislation proposed and the programs suggested have only superficially related the issues. One cannot deal with energy independently of money or vice versa. The analyses, as made by the several interested protagonists and antagonists, are not satisfying to many trained in economic analysis.

But more significantly there seems to be a failure to deal with and control the particular problems at hand. For example, while it is acknowledged that raising the price of gasoline will curtail its use, no realistic provision is made or even considered for lower income people, who in the post–World War 2 period have developed a pattern of living far from the workplace. To speak of public transport as a solution is fairly nonsensical, because the United States has only a vestigial public transport system. Nor has the West Coast surplus of Alaskan oil been considered.

Other issues are closely related to the energy-monetary problem. The pollution problem is one. If coal becomes a more important energy substitute, issues of a technological and capital supply nature will arise. If technology and capital are subsidized, on whom will the subsidy fall as a cost, and what effect will the new arrangements have on prices, interest rates, and the savings-investment ratio to GNP? (Household and probably business savings are low in relation to GNP as compared to even the recent past.)

It sounds as if one is suggesting total planning on the logic that the head bone is connected to the neck bone, and the back bone is connected, etc. for that is the way of the Lord. But our intent is not to support total planning, indeed rather to urge it be avoided. Our suggestion is that issues, public policies, and programs fall into associated groupings. The state of economic and social analysis, in the main, permits reasonable definitions of such groupings. Each must be considered more or less simultaneously if serious omissions and breakdowns are to be avoided. The limited generalization is the ideal in *explicitly* setting goals. The implicit goal setting mechanism probably never worked, but surely is not relevant in a complex world which requires intervention. Explicit goals however can be set, and the means to them analyzed with at least modest success, we believe.

One of the means, as we suggested earlier, is to leave well enough alone. This is to suggest relying on the automatic functioning of markets insofar as possible. Where interference is required, policy should be to interfere as little as possible, to relieve the hindrances on the market mechanism so as to let it function. This is not a universal rule, since positive intervention is often necessary to attain a goal, e.g., education, affirmative action, but the issues should be thought through, and the programs carefully scrutinized by knowledgeable people whose interests and commitments are not involved.

We argue that the great role of management is to adjust its organization and behavior to the future. This means that direction of the firm, and the connections with its markets, constantly undergo change. The manager's task is to maneuver his firm and try to control its environment. The internal architecture and structuring of the enterprise also should be adjusted to the new forces, whether market-generated as technology, or governmentally generated as policy. Business managers and their technical advisers, including legal advisers, would be in a better position to make decisions if they knew better what was happening, and had opportunity to comment on it.[5]

The more complex the business world becomes, the less meaningful do general rules and detailed regulations seem. Particular cases and circumstances require particular restraints. This is a big task. But at issue are very serious questions which affect the lives and fortunes of millions of people, and the strength of the republic. Few ethical issues are greater.

This advice, no doubt, would be difficult to follow. But goodness and effectiveness are not easily won. Restraint is a social virtue, for nothing is done from which some effect does not follow.

Good results are, as we know, rare in government intervention. So long as markets work, let them work. When business performance is not reasonable, only then should ways be sought to improve the situation.

6

SHOULD I TELL MY PARTNER?
Justice, Morality, Ethics

Senator Kefauver, once head of a Senate committee pursuing the butterfly of ethics, recounted the story of a businessman who described the ethical dilemma as follows:

> I own a store and one day I was tending the store and a customer came in and bought some goods and paid for it with a twenty dollar bill. Through an honest mistake I gave him change only for a ten dollar bill. This confronted me with an ethical problem in business. *Should I tell my partner about that extra ten dollars?*

All of which summarizes poignantly a major ethical problem. To whom do we owe ethical behavior, and if it comes to a tradeoff, to whose ethical values should we adhere? It might even be proposed with some merit that ethics is more a matter of skilled decision making, in the face of uncertainty in an imperfect world, than of saintly other worldliness.

This anecdote also illustrates the significance of context in determining the meaning, hence definitions of morality and ethics. The relation between the seller and the buyer, the one who unwittingly overpaid, is skipped over as irrelevant. The petty merchant has no obligation to him. The tone of the story makes the buyer "a pigeon" for the seller. From the viewpoint of the pigeon, if he knew, an injustice has been done him, he has been bilked. But his viewpoint is not at issue. The context of the tale concentrates on the relation between the partners, and on that alone. Does not convention require reciprocal honesty between partners? Do virtue and morality require the sharing of windfall gains, when either partner alone, is aware of the windfall?

Morality, justice, and ethics have different meanings for different people, and in different circumstances. Nevertheless we do live with some tolerable harmony in a society. This means there is constant interaction directly—person-to-person—or indirectly through institutions, often via markets. Interest in social conflict is, in some fashion, the recognition that (1) conflict is not all-embracing, the world is not chaotic, and (2) conflict is assumed to be, in many if not all instances, reducible. Social harmony as the goal of human behavior is implicit in a great fraction of social theorizing.[1]

Most people measure behavior as good in at least two senses: (1) a desired goal is achieved by the behavior, and (2) the behavior and the goal are not in violation of what behaviors and goals ought to be. The "ought" is, of course, a nonlogical stumbling block. What ought to be, or how a person or society ought to go about reducing unemployment or inflation, or rewarding productivity or goodness, are issues which may divide a society, even a society of experts. The informed disagreements on what the economy ought to be, and how to achieve the alternatively suggested goals, make up a great deal of the substance of the workings and thinking of professional economists and politicians.

We cannot get around this choice of ends without relying on an absolute, nonreducible *set* of values. Fortunately in an ongoing society the debate about absolutes is often made unnecessary because many nonreducible constraints, or their surrogates, are already deeply imbedded in social thought and behavior. After all, many values of society are very persistent. Obedience to, or respect for, conventions takes the place of justifying every act by an appeal to some absolute. When basic or essential values or conventions are not generally accepted but require frequent justification, then the society is in trouble, or is in a revolutionary, transitional phase. When acceptance of a norm or value set is general, then no problems need be faced on that score.

New means or new goals, or both, do not, of themselves, usually present moral problems to society. New technology may cause unemployment, or new ends may be shoddy products or even harmful ones. To a surprising extent however ordinary market forces bring about corrections. New enterprises, new products, and new technologies fail more often than they succeed. It is the successes, the persistent innovations, which bring both benefit and trouble to society. The issues which simply do not disappear are the ones which require conscious moral choice. A major task of this chapter is to suggest a typology of ethics which will be of assistance in classifying and differentiating various kinds of business behavior from the ethical viewpoint. To make the analysis flow, the general term ethics will be used in the immediately following discussion. The structure also fits justice and morality. The typology is, needless to say, an exercise in definition making. Similarly conventions have contextual meaning or definition. Often conventions are enacted into law, but the question of context or relevance persists.

Definitions stand pretty much on their own. However if a definition is self contradictory like containing or implying a square circle, it is nonsensical, which is to say not operational. The concern with non-operational definitions and words is one which plagues economics and other ordered, orderly discussions of every day events and behavior. Alice's query about who is the master, we or the words, is a sound, logical question. We, sometimes the speaker, and sometimes a collection of people, are the boss of words and hence definitions which if used *out of a social context,* have no meaning. But we always operate *in* a social context. Meaning or definition is related to usage, which is to say some common agreement.

But how confusing is usage. Profits for example, is a word of nearly every day use. But "profits are up 100 percent this quarter," is a different concept from asserting "profits are an unnecessary payment which may adhere to any factor of production." Or the idea that profits contain a major source of self investible funds for a corporation is a different notion from profits being the wage of management, or profits being the difference between selling prices and wages which tend to a subsistence level. All these ideas have some notion that profits are a differential rate or difference between income and one or more kinds of cost. But profits has to be defined for each context to be meaningful.

We know, and not so very deep down, that laws are not always expected to be obeyed, so that conventional behavior may supplant the law as enacted or judicially stated. This may account for the dynamics of the Common Law. But even in trivial and not so trivial matters, legislated enactments are not always exactly followed, as in the 55 miles per hour speed limit, or in the legal limit of payment by coin generally being waived in small consumer purchases. Even jail sentences rarely mean what they say, and the Xerox machine has changed copyright restrictions. The rule of convention taking the place of enacted legislation occurs in the "past practice" rule in collective bargaining, and in other circumstances often, or perhaps usually, where not very much is at stake, and the persons involved are aware of the conventions. When the chips are down however the enacted law will be the rule followed.

But our point is that convention or law embrace and define most of the interactions between and among people. We swim in a sea of convention, law and contract, which we may call rule. Adherence to rule is what is expected. It is going *beyond* the requirement of rule for the benefit of another party or person, that one, the doer, may in our rubric, be considered as praiseworthy, or ethical. (This is not unlike an aspect of the Christian ethic.)

Where the rules which constrain the doer of the deed into behavior which the observer finds unethical by his standards, or by the standards (conventional values) of the society at large or a large segment of it, then the constraining law or convention may be at fault and unjust or immoral. If, as is asserted but not proved, the federal minimum wage law causes unemployment among youth and minority groups, and the current convention of the society makes employment a paramount good, then the law is unethical and just plain bad. If nuclear energy carries great and irreducible risks for miners, workers, users, and third parties, and no one knows what to do with the waste products to reduce their dangerous emissions, then nuclear energy may be a social bad, regardless of law or argument. Actions supportive of such energy then are unethical. In each case there are *implications* of the particular activity, minimum wages or nuclear energy, which must be considered in an evaluation. The point we are making is that the constraints on behavior, legal and conventional, are more likely to contain ethical ingredients than the particular activities themselves.

In business conventional behavior is to a remarkable extent legislated. Where business disobeys the law the issue may be ethical, but usually it is less ethical than legal, for both correction and legitimation are in the law. It is almost like double jeopardy to convict a person of an illegal act, and at the same time of an unethical one. To be sure, we hasten to add, illegal acts may be unethical. Obloquy may result from flying in the face of legal or social constraints. But if the law requires an act, or at least does not prohibit an act which has untoward social implications, the law is as much at fault as the perpetrator of the act.

The ethics of business behavior is then difficult to determine from the viewpoint of the manager. Is law a superior force or are his ethical leanings superior, other things being equal. In the generality of cases, law seems the better of the two, from the general social viewpoint.

The context we are concerned with is business and the business manager as business and manager. Producing, buying, selling, planning for the market is the context of the definitions. But the concern cannot stop there, and definitions will have to be changed in the light of the new contexts to which the argument flows. Actions have repercussions and implications beyond the immediate.

Let us consider a hypothetical Three Mile Island nuclear plant. We shall call it Big N (BN). BN was organized by a group, let us assume, that thought it could make money as a public utility. All the various forms, certifications, hearings, proofs of reliability, and necessity were complied with to the letter, and even to the spirit. The license was granted. The plant was built, again with regard to the provisions of law and regulation. There is a gala opening and the plant goes to work. Up to now external constraints on the firm were the major legal requirements.

Suddenly the well ordered plant goes awry, and a Three Mile Island dysfunction occurs. The firm denies responsibility, claiming it obeyed the rules, and had no knowledge that the rules were not sufficient to assure safe operation. But regardless of what the company claims by way of self exoneration, and regardless of what the state or federal officials aver, there is an enormous danger to half the state and more, and there are implications for consumers, producers, buyers, and, in short, people and property far beyond the BN region.

The context of our interest has changed. Right, wrong, ethical, unethical have to be redefined in the light of the changed concerns.

If the firm, BN, knew that the rules it was following were not appropriate, from the viewpoint of safety the firm, given the nature of the undertaking, was committing a most unethical act. But let us suppose that it was in ignorance of the truth. The firm relied on "higher authority" as it were. Then, it would seem that the "higher authority" had the responsibility of pushing its search for knowledge and its regulations to the margin of the state of the art, and even beyond, by developing new knowledge. Ignorance becomes less an ethical defense as the implications of an act become more costly, widespread and horrendous, and as the firm has a greater resource of knowledge.

We assert then, that obedience to law, by business is a necessary requirement, with the proviso that, if the firm has knowledge of the law being socially dysfunctional, it promptly bring such information to the attention of the proper authorities, and correct its own behavior.

But our concern, or major concern, is not with the law, which is the ethical statement of the society through the administration, courts and legislature. Our concern is with business and its behavior. Rules determined outside the firm are as given for the firm. The implications of business behavior, and the legitimation of business as an institution are where the great ethical and moral issues lie.

A great significance is to be found in differentiating among the several levels of legitimation of behavior. The three levels of legitimation which we have chosen are:

1. The Minimal Ethic—where the firm interacts with relatively small opposite numbers—e.g., an employee or employees as individuals, a buyer or a seller

2. The Big Ethic—where the firm interacts with other institutions in a market, e.g., sharing in market decisions or trade union contract decisions

3. The Grand Ethic—where the firm, through the business institution, is directly interacting with other institutions, including governmental ones, to determine, change, or effect the legal rules and institutions of the society.

The Minimal Ethic is not small in terms of the frequency of its involvement, nor of the significance to those involved. It is called minimal because typically a single or few individuals are up against an economic power of great resource, a corporation or large institution. It is David the small against Goliath the big. Ethics is concerned with determining, or criticizing, conduct in the light of notions of goodness, right, or welfare. Ethics is, in the view presented here, imbedded in time, place, and situation. It is not an absolute. It comes into being out of the pull and tug of events, and reflects the capacity of an actor to control the events in the light of his values and ideals. But ethical behavior is not a mere habit or convention, for then there is little conscious contribution by the actor; *ethics is nothing if it is not volitional.* This implies that ethical behavior is the child of goodness of kindness and power, for goodness without the power to accomplish something is a mere phrase; and power without the concept of goodness is a constant threat to all of lesser power.

Ethics deals with the distribution of power and wealth as part of its concern. Ideas of behavior come out of the realities of life, and are legitimations of individual or institutional behavior. In the tradition of Great Britain and America—indeed in the modern tradition of the Western world—social ethics has been seen as a practical force governed by institutional, which is to say social, values.[2] To suggest that a leader is doctrinaire, an ideologue, is to cast suspicion on the leader. The criticism suggests that the leader is not practical, and/or does not see the complex of values but only a singular value.

The smallest unit in a workplace is an individual. It is with such a unit that all moral considerations begin, and often end. The decision to change the work week, because of considerations of efficiency, may satisfy the needs of the manager and his fiscal situation, but may play havoc with the family life of the employees. A Grand Ethic agreement on how to ration or otherwise distribute gasoline, agreed to by officials of government, oil industry and White House appointed spokesmen for the public, might work great hardship on many families who could not possibly have been consulted, and were they consulted have had but little to contribute to the solution of the problem.

The typology we suggest helps to classify the questions of business ethics, but it does lend an improper suggestion that the classification somehow mirrors the reality. Not so. Ultimately all ethical issues affect individuals and families. But the issues, in the first instance, must be classified, lest analytic chaos result.

The ensuing discussion, then, is not rigidly cast into three parts— minimal, big, and grand ethics. To a degree the discussion tends to consider all levels as the argument develops. However the stress at the onset is in the Minimal, moving to the Big and ending with the Grand Ethic. There is a methodological justification for the loose approach. If we made a set of strict definitions, adhered to them with rigor, and applied a faultless logic, that is one not concerned with the alternatives of reality, then the conclusions would probably not be very interesting nor useful in explaining reality or suggesting guides for action. On the other hand looser definitions applied with a concern of how reality operates might well provide a range of conclusions with a high probability of fruitful application. It is the latter approach which we have elected to use.

It is naive to believe that if all people were of good will and dedication all interpersonal and social issues would be harmoniously and agreeably solved. Such a view is naive because people, as individuals and groups, have different as well as conflicting interests; and are convinced that they have rights, often privileges, in particular solutions. In a world of scarce resources, interests conflict. Where the market can adjust these differences via the pricing system, all is well. But individuals and groups are typically of unequal power economically, politically, and by other measures; then power comes into play. But power requires legitimation.[3]

We often make a distinction between power and force, as in market force and power. Power is centered in a person or institution, whereas force is impersonal and uncentered. It is purposive. Where power distribution in a market (or elsewhere if we are interested in non-market phenomena) is markedly unequal, so that one person or group has great advantages over other persons or groups, then the stability of the resulting relationship can scarcely be called harmonious. My paying a monopoloid price, or what I consider a monopoloid price, for a prescribed drug is a transaction. It is, however, no proof or measure of the harmony or goodwill I feel for the druggist or manufacturer who set the price. Whether or not I am justified is not at issue. The point is that a transaction completed does not indicate a harmonious, satisfactory relationship between buyer and seller. Even in competitive markets the "harmony" of the market may be, and probably would be, more apparent than realized. The exercise of power, in a market, is almost guaranteed to create dissatisfaction.

A shipbuilding firm's notice that time clocks would be placed near the hull to be worked on, and not at the gate, was honored at first. But soon the employees began to discuss the matter, and without referring to grievance simply called a wildcat strike. The issue of walking a quarter mile from gate to hull, and thus having to be at work fifteen minutes earlier than in the past, was the ostensible reason for the wildcat strike. The real reason, investigation revealed, was that no one in the local union had been consulted, and so the company action was viewed as the naked exercise of power. Had the local union been consulted, or had a grievance been filed, so that the orderly, ordered mechanism for settling differences been used, then market (and contractual) force would have been brought to bear in the ensuing discussion, and market power would not have been the cause for dissension.

Force, or market force, as we use the term, implies an ordered adjustive mechanism often leading to equilibrium (in physics and economics). Power is the imposition of a rule. In a market of sale and purchase, force, or market force, is a synonym for competition, as in "forces of competition." Power, on the other hand, tends to be the reliance on unlegitimated authority, as in monopoly power.

The shipbuilding example given above is to illustrate a real or potential conflict between two parties, here bound by a contract, each of whose resources are considerable. The social dangers implicit in their disagreement, as in a strike or lockout, or in a conflict causing ship buyers to go to other yards and so to inflict injury on the inhabitants of the community, are obvious. Trade union vs industry examples are easy to come by, and often are exciting. But other market exercises of power to impose order are equally significant. The age of the robber barons involves historical memories of the exercise of power fomenting trouble, even evil. In our own day the use of political power to restrict imports because foreign producers of steel and shoes sell at lower price than American firms entails obvious social mischief in the market process and efficient allocation of resources. The power of the energy industry, in its various facets too, has triggered criticism and claims of social injury.

In the popular mind large scale industry, enormous government, big unions, and financial giantism have made the impersonality of market decisions suspect. The financial success of physicians, business managers, tennis players and other professional athletes, ex-government servants, and the families of current government officials—the list is endless—has planted seeds of doubt. Does the market really work effectively and efficiently to allocate scarce resources to their best use, or is power, subtle or crude, a significant factor in determining what makes the system work—for the private and selfish interests of those on the inside?[4]

Power in the market, and power in the making of rules are easily seen as being the potential sources of unethical, immoral, and unjust business behavior. Market power and power in forcing a compromise may generate conventions and rules which legitimate behavior which, when judged by other standards of the society are outside the pale of social legitimation which rests on broader and more deeply rooted moral and ethical bases. Injustice is the final result, for the individual has little defense against the apparently legitimate power of the firm.

Who makes the rules and laws by which the economy is supposed to work?[5] If government regulators are themselves regulated by those they are supposed to control, clearly something is wrong. Yet the charge that government regulation is often dominated by the firms and industries being regulated is a frequent one. Indeed congressional hearings from time to time tend to support the contention. Incomes policy—that is, price and wage controls as practiced in the United States, either as "jawbone" or with sanctions—has not been without its critics. The cost overrun scandals in government procurement, the market behavior of major electrical manufacturing companies in the notorious market sharing and price fixing case of the 1960s cast doubt on the morality of some business. The charges of hanky-panky in intraindustry sales and purchase during the 1973–74 and 1978–79 oil crises are examples of real or claimed antisocial policies of industry and government. It is not strange that the government is always present as a force supporting reasonable behavior or as a force supporting improper action. In large scale activity government cannot, by the nature of things, be totally absent.

It would be a grievous error if the reader were left with the impression that, when large agencies such as business, government, or trade unions devise public policy by legislation or other agreement, antisocial results inevitably follow and private interests alone are protected. Much legislation and many agreements and understandings, hopefully the vast majority of both, reflect the values of the society. It is sad but not surprising that not all attempts to achieve harmony or at least goodness are successful. The world is extremely complex and unstable, while knowledge and capacity to control are somewhat limited. In good times and bad those with economic power undoubtedly try to adjust their differences and suggest policies and programs to solve or alleviate pressing social problems. That each power tries to protect itself is not an indictment. That many do not use their entire power to win a point—that is, that compromise occurs—is obvious to anyone who has observed or assisted at the creation of policy.

The relation between the firm and an individual is our first concern. In such a limited case it is quite clear that the power of contending parties is not always, nor even often likely to be equal. There is therefore the easy opportunity for a firm to use its power indiscriminately. Of course, there are often legal limits. Then the power is restrained; and restrained power is diluted power. But often, perhaps usually, legal restraints are ineffective because of the money cost and risk the aggrieved party need pay to the law. Also there is often a tendency for an aggrieved person, for one reason or another, to nurse the grievance but not to contend; or even to be ignorant of the nature of his exploitation.

Realistically one does not sue a drug manufacturer, or bring a complaint for apparent violations of sections 1 and 2 of the Sherman Act, or of section 7 of the Clayton Act, because one is paying too much for a pill. In such circumstance legal protection for an individual is out of the question. The best one can hope for is relief via some other person's appeal to the legislature or the courts, with someone else paying the costs. If such a suit is successful, correction will be imposed by the power of legal and government authority and so will be out of the realm of the ethical as we have defined it. To be sure, insofar as the legal action and law reflect the values of the society, both plaintiff and society are better off, so in a sense justice and morality, hence ethics, have been served.

But let us look at an issue from another angle. A firm has authority and power to hire and fire, with only minor legal restraint. A worker habitually comes in five or ten minutes late. The personnel department calls the worker in for a talk and discovers that he has a sick wife, five young children, and relatively little skill. The wife and children are so situated that lateness is virtually inevitable. Should the worker be dismissed?

The moral and ethical question has to do with the exercise of power in the light of practicality and institutional and conventional values. From the viewpoint of the embattled employee he is asking for justice. What are the implications of the alternative acts? The failure to dismiss may induce other employees to be tardy. Then costs and returns are involved. If dismissal would raise the ire of other workers who are sympathetic to the hard luck fellow, another scenario may be written. Other implications need to be considered in the light of the probable effects. Then a decision can be reasonably made. The several implications construct the nature of the decision and action. Power has to be restrained in the light of the welfare of the firm and employee. If the employee is retained, power, in a sense, has been diffused through its distribution to the weaker party. Harmony, in at least a limited sense, has been achieved. Presumably the disharmony which might have arisen from the employee's not being fired is lessened even if there is some residual disharmony in not firing him. The employee's being retained generates less disharmony than would his being fired. The issue was not treated legalistically, nor mechanically. Power was tempered with goodness, and the result was generosity, but also at lower social cost to the firm and other employees. Justice was done the employee. But this is only one of many possible scenarios.

The ethical behavior by the manager, which is to say the firm, is a combination of morality and justice. In our language this represents behavior toward a person of lesser power and authority which the person considers fair or appropriate. The manager may, even will, see his actions as kind and good. Ethics also has the component of morality— that is, going beyond what the ideology requires in a given circumstance.

To act justly one must be able to imagine what the person of lesser power conceives as his due, or what is fair. Adam Smith used the word "sympathy" to define the feeling that one with power, or an observer, feels. By this feeling one may understand the values, expectations, and situation of the person with the small power and authority. We should, in our times, more likely use the word "empathy" to describe such feeling.

To do justice—that is, to act positively on the basis of empathy—
is often restricted by law, convention, and self-interest. To act morally
is similarly constrained, although the legal and conventional constraints
are different, to the extent that behavior of a firm toward another
firm differs from the behavior of a firm to an employee.

The expectations of competition in a competing firm's behavior
are more likely to be expectations of the behavior of an equal in
power than if an individual is involved. Differing degrees of power
and authority may be graded from single person to great corporation.
When questions of ethics and morality become less pressing than the
search for market strategies, the market power of the competitor
with which the firm in question is engaged comes into play. The
more powerful the opponent, the more steadfast one must be. The
weaker the opponent, the more lenient. The rule works both ways.
Thus, in a sense, the idea of justice may be expanded from the expectation or the self-determined conception of a single person to that
of the bigger entity, the corporation. The firm and the single employee
want their due—justice.

The layer of ethical decisions we have been discussing is only one
of three. It may be considered the tier of the Minimal ethic, as compared to the other two. Generosity is a virtue in those who can exercise power. But generosity is restrained by the consideration of its implications. The generous fool, or generous short-sighted sympathetic
soul, may produce more trouble and social disharmony than the powerful person who sticks closely to the rule, the convention, and the contract. But the generous, powerful firm or person who examines the
alternatives and unifies them in the light of a general view of welfare
is exercising justice, both power and goodness. Hence such actions are
ethical. The trick is to be correct in one's analysis of the implications
of alternative actions, and to take into account the reactions and
values of those affected. Then wisdom is wedded to ethics and justice.

"The Good" is an idealization. That man strives or should strive
for the good is idealistic or poetic; unless some guidelines for behavior
are available. Some hint as to what he should be doing are vital. "Good"
or "the Good" contains the same word as the prosaic word "goods."

And herein lies a dilemma. The good life, or doing good, in the abstractions of many, perhaps most, people, is divorced from the notion that such a life should be paid off by an inundation of rewards in the form of income. The opposite view is one generally held that commendable behavior is rewarded by an inner glow, a feeling of accomplishment which money cannot buy. Virtue is its own reward. So although we conceive goods as things which can be bought and sold, the ultimate in good presumably is the sum of the essences of all goods, and is beyond price and market. Reflection on this shift in the content of the word is confusing.

In the modern world many people see the great ethical conflict as between democracy (and private capitalism) on the one hand and communism (and public capital) on the other. The ideal—the poetic Good for both societies—is related, inter alia, to physical goods, i.e., income. Both have a materialistic orientation in terms of their goals. They may differ as to questions of ownership and distribution but not as to questions of physical technology. Both societies want to maximize the social dividend while minimizing costs. The institutional and practical forms, the modalities of ownership and control—in brief, the nonphysical technological environmental biases—of each society are assumed to be ideally different. And herein lies the reduction of the dilemma.

It is the *means* of acquiring goods and allocating resources which differs for the two societies. Means, as opposed to ends, should be amenable to rational discussion. But alas no! Neither the spokesmen nor the societal high priests of either society are willing, or perhaps able, to argue that what are significant are the means, the institutions, rather than the goals. But *the way to get a good is a great part, often the major portion, of the Good.*[6]

But this observation also applies to smaller situations. How many university administrators and professors, all dedicated to learning and truth, inquire as to the government funds which are available for what purposes, and then design research to attract the money? Business, on the other hand, overtly is more likely to examine the market and try to produce for the market. University research should not be equated to selling shoes or underwear. University research is often sold on the basis of prestige and as being scientifically urgent, although its genesis may have been in the public budget. This is doubtless as true in the Soviet Union as in the United States. Both universities and businesses in the United States learn to operate in the market, constrained by the rules and practices considered appropriate in the market in question.

Thus for the second layer of ethical and moral decisions—the Big Ethic—institutional behavior in the market is an important consideration, as important as profits, salability, and perpetuity. Many years ago Sumner Slichter, then professor of economics at Harvard, pointed out that factories turn out people as well as goods. The people, both blue and white collar personnel, are affected by their jobs and the psychological and social aura surrounding the workplace. Business then must be judged on what it does to and for people, as a significant test of its output.

The mere election (by a scant majority of voters and a minority of potential dues paying members) of a collective bargaining agent at a large university, within a week had the provost talking about management prerogatives as if he knew what these ephemeral rights were. The starry eyed (nondues paying) faculty were talking about the rewards the union would bring. The good life for unsophisticated administrators and faculty alike became redefined by the existence of a new morality. To the teachers a new means had been created, a means of (hopefully) incredible efficacy. To the administrators a new factor had been introduced which somehow enhanced administration and converted it to management. Of course, time corrected the corruption of novelty, but things never were the same again. Once utopian ideal is embraced, it leaves its mark.

In business, more cost and returns oriented than universities, similar results have sometimes followed collective bargaining elections. The institutionalization of collective bargaining in its current form after the 1930s however has resulted in a more realistic set of attitudes. The current attitudes have tended to harden into conventional behavior which can be upset only with risk to the firm and the union. Similarly new technology affects the making of wage schedules and job structure, as well as expectations. Often no great ethical or moral problems are involved in such second tier adjustments, because neither the Minimal Ethic (generosity) nor the Grand Ethic (compromise) is involved. Rather, institutional groupings are involved, and the adjustments, while of course operating through individuals, are really habits of thought and therefore institutional in their nature.

Such situations usually require consideration of how best to introduce a novel set of behavior patterns (i.e., the more economizing constraints). "Social engineering," a term popular after World War 2, comprehends the idea of adjustive planning. Ethical considerations may arise if the adjustments are known or imagined to be injurious to health—either consumer or employee health—or are likely to be the cause of something untoward such as a wholesale business dislocation.

During the early days of World War 2, the rubber industry was running out of new rubber, so new synthetics were being introduced. The introduction was costly and hurried. Synthetics had not been market tested, nor were the manufacturing processes without the bugs that so often infest new procedures. Workers in the Akron mechanical rubber goods plants petitioned the government for assistance because the new synthetics, it was alleged, were causing skin disease (or worse), and sterility among women.

Two eminent industrial physicians were called in by the government, one from Harvard Medical School the other from New York City's Health Department. After a two day investigation of hundreds of employees and virtually all the rubber shops, the two experts agreed that:

1. the time span since the introduction of the synthetics was not sufficient to judge whether female sterility was increasing;

2. there was no reason to believe that skin irritations, or any other untoward effects, arose from handling the synthetics;

3. that the solvents used smelt differently from the solvents normally used to bond and glue rubber, and this olfactory novelty was upsetting to the workforce.

The solution was to bring in a number of large fans and place new air vents in the factories. The issue simply ceased to be, after concern was openly shown and some minor physical changes made. If the government had followed the advice of the union, which was screaming bloody murder, or of industry, which insisted everything was fine, war production might have been delayed for many months. Justice, morality, and ethics were assured by the interested parties acting in the direction of common sense ideology—ascertaining the facts. The point of the example is that if problems arise in business which involve institutional adjustments, rules of contract and common sensical social adjustment need to be followed to cater to conceptions of ethical or moral requirement.

The same holds for other market situations. A contract, agreed to by the parties involved, is not carved in stone. There are orderly ways to amend, change, and even get out from under onerous contracts or those whose provisions were unwisely prepared. Society has even provided for bankruptcy procedures. In other words, there are orderly ways to react to adverse market forces.

To exercise market power under the guise of ethical requirement is to introduce into an ordered system a feature whose effects may be untoward not only to the contracting parties but to others. Besides, when the issues are very weighty, one can easily summon market power and justify it as doing good. The public discussion of American investments in South Africa is a case in point. Industry often tries to justify its continued presence there by asserting that blacks benefit. Critics argue that industry is supporting apartheid. No one seems concerned that each is trying to make foreign policy without recourse to government. To force, by public pressure, a firm out of South Africa means that forcing a firm out of Great Britain, or the Soviet Union or Quebec, is possibly legitimated, and so foreign economic policy of the United States is being made outside the government. This is a dangerous course of action, even for those who, like the present writer, abhor apartheid.

In the market, forces should be allowed to operate freely so long as such untrammeled behavior doesn't result in socially untoward results. This is the ethical way if markets are to continue as functioning institutions. In this regard, the second level activities are different from the first level and third level activities. In our thinking, the market institution is one of the many which interact to make society what it is. Government, for all its majesty, is but an interactive institution, with a legal monopoly on violence. This is probably one of the reasons that the Founding Fathers divided governance into three separate compartments. We have intragovernment interaction as well as government interaction with other institutions.

The use of social and ethical arguments designed to frustrate market behavior in the name of social responsibility is often a social abuse.

Many people, conservative, liberal, and radical, have asserted that moral arguments have been used to hide downright conspiracy, or worse, in the guise of consumer, labor, or small business protection. Minimum wage laws were originally attacked—often by trade unionists—because the minima would become maxima. Pure food and drug rules have been attacked because they solidify the position of firms already in the market. Election reform laws are criticized because they are more protective of incumbents than of challengers. Income policies (wage and price controls) are opposed because they tend to "freeze" firms and trade unions into preferred positions. Monetary or fiscal reform are critically examined in the light of their rewards (or disbenefits) to particular segments of the economy. Examples of criticisms or doubts about the ethical validity of policy can be multiplied. That many interventions have had unfortunate and often unexpected results is a truism.

What the criticisms tend to illuminate is (1) the insecurity felt in some quarters over the correctness of economic or social analysis and (2) the diversity of interests in the bodies public and economic. Regulatory agencies or government administration—e.g., public utility commissions, building code administrations, various federal and state rate making bodies, the Food and Drug Administration—all have been accused, seemingly with reason and merit, of sometimes acting in the interest of those whom they were organized to regulate. The bawdy song of our youth which began "Who takes care of the caretaker's daughter when the caretaker's busy taking care?" has a ring of truth when generalized to the market.

This should not be taken to mean that market laissez faire is a realizable ideal.[7] Often control or government regulation *is* desirable. But it should be frequently reviewed, and its implications thoroughly examined, on an ongoing basis.

If firms in a market are many and with approximately equal market power then competition works well. In the process which is bounded by law and convention, an essential ingredient is the conception of self-interest. Survival and well being are the sine qua non of decision making and behavior, with bankruptcy a reasonable, indeed, moral, end should business survival otherwise require illegal or immoral behavior.

Morality and justice may well imply compromises by the manager to legitimize his behavior in his own eyes and in the public conception. If a firm is polluting the atmosphere, and attention is called to the action, the firm has a number of alternatives. It can argue, inter alia, that no law is being broken, or that the cost of antipollution devices is so high that their installation is out of the question. Also the threat of unemployment is obvious. But if a serious issue is squarely faced, and a workable solution sought, regardless of the outcome, toil and ultimate trouble are likely to be minimized. If the firm, recognizing the seriousness and validity of a complaint, sets about correcting the pollutive situation, it may avoid legislation which might have been more restrictive and costly. If the firm recognizes the implications of its behavior, finds the solution not costly beyond its capacity, and corrects the situation, it gains good will. Good will is an asset, and good will growing out of self-imposed restraint on power is a social good, with ethical overtones. If the firm succeeds in doing nothing and is not in violation of law, it is nevertheless behaving immorally and unethically, in our view.

The Grand Ethic, the statement of public policy and the provision, insofar as possible, of the social means to accomplish the public purpose, is not to be found in a law book. True, the laws of the land— laws regulating, requiring, and limiting social and individual activity— are often negations; but they expose, often by implication, a portion of the ideals of the society. But laws and compromises are also positively stated and insist "Thou shalt." "Thou shalt not," by restricting behavior (often by implication), tells us what is expected. Sections 1 and 2 of the Sherman Act, by denying the right to monopolize by inference recommend competition. Minimum wages are set by law as often are liquor prices. Consent decrees define and restrict behavior, and so regulation is a positive and a negative way of life.

The Good, however is rarely overtly stated as an ultimate goal or hierarchy of goals. The Good is more vague than that, and contains conflicting and mutually exclusive components. Competition is a good in the Good, but so is more income or the protection of the economically weak. The concerns might not always have compatible solutions. Freedom from want (guaranteed annual income?) is a good, but so is private property in producer as well as consumer goods. The rights of property (whatever they may be) clearly might conflict with human rights. Neither is an absolute, nor is either defined for all time. Such intermediate ideals as art, education and medical care are costly, very costly if indulged. Yet such social needs and ideas, if accomplished, must divert income and wealth from other efforts, which from time to time become very insistent. The cost of national defense in general can have no upper limits, if factions of the arms industry or the military are to be taken seriously. Also medical care, education, welfare, etc., according to the proponents of these ideal goods, are almost without a ceiling. Utopia or the Good as an ideal is not only a complex, changing hierarchy of goals, whose change cannot be foretold, but the content of the Good is interpreted differently by various people who tend to support many of the same ideals.

In opposition to certain ideals Women's Libbers, young men of draft age, some blacks, and other fractionated groups joined together in the revolution of the sixties. Their goal was nothing less than to change the system and disestablish the Establishment, without the new ideal being defined. This is not to denigrate the attempt, for even Marx is reputed to have said, when asked about the revolutionary future, "I cannot give you of the recipes of the cookshops of the future." However it is apparent the befuddled flower children had little in common with the Black Panthers, or Women's Lib with the Weathermen, as the late 1970s saw. Social criticism, like politics, makes strange bedfellows.

Yet deep in the American society there is something like a consensus, or persistent ideology. (J. J. Rousseau saw it as the "General Will"): Not everyone shares all of it, but most people accept various parts of it. Individual freedom, not entirely unrestrained, is desirable and is linked in some ways to a belief in political democracy. This may not be a blueprint of social structure, but it is sufficient to set constraints on government. In situations where private business power seems distressing, the general will is enough to justify surface concerns that at least a modest standard of life and freedom should be assured everyone, no matter how stupid, unlucky, or foolish the individual is. The general will seems to support, say, an anti-trust policy, whose major virtue seems to be a profound objection to the concentration of economic power. But there is also the deep seated belief that big industrial units produce goods more cheaply than smaller units, and more goods are better than fewer.

The vague ideals, the deep, hidden beliefs are not shared by everyone. Under the pressures of living national politics, personal, social, and moral biases, values, and the visions of the world held by individuals, especially sensitive people, change. When politicians, the press, or self-conscious citizens reflect on the human condition, values change, and older virtues are often replaced by newer ones. For color conscious blacks who feel socially exploited and left out of the mainstream, the utopian and basic ideological feelings are stated in different words and maybe even with slightly different meanings from the words of a WASP newspaper editor, or a big city, middle class intellectual. But the thrust is often the same—limitations on the power and capacity of those in seats of authority, and more freedom, power, and status for those who are being pushed around or neglected. To be sure, there is no general agreement as to what class is in power and authority, or what class should be helped. (Classes are hard to define in any general sense.) There is even less agreement on how power and wealth should be redistributed. One of the most pathetic slogans of the revolutionary left is "Power to the People." Which people, what power, how is power transferred? Only idiots can take such a slogan seriously.

Ideologies, especially deep seated values, are usually not operational. The doing, the legislating, the policy and program preparing, all provide a number of different ideologic twists and interpretations. Was the Fair Labor Standards Act passed to keep some people out of the labor market, or was it enacted to assure the employed poor better income? Either side can be argued. Possibly the proponents of the act were, and still are, not clear on the point. But the supporters and the critics agree, in general, that there is a social concern with the poor. That is the deep rooted ideological force. The remainder is technique. The great arguments in society are more often over technique than over ideals.

The interests, values, and goals of individuals and groups, institutionalized (e.g., U.S. Manufacturers Association, AFL-CIO, Gay Liberation movement) or more haphazardly put together (e.g., the Anti-Vietnam movement or Ban the Throwaway Bottle movement) vary widely. The reactions of such groups to the issues which caused the movements to be born are usually fairly obvious. The Manufacturers' Association will take the position on the National Labor Relations Act which one might expect, even if one knows only the general issues being discussed. Similarly the AFL-CIO's position might be correctly guessed.

Knee jerk liberal and conservative reactions are not rare in the modern world. But when the issues are subtle or where the analysis is not obvious, the decisions are not easily guessed, or foretellable at all, and the implications of alternative decisions are vague. Inflation arouses more than ideological or class interests. Monetary policy, like abortion, generates interest which cuts across economic class lines.

The views and analytic expectations of sophisticated lawyers, scholars, individual businessmen, or trade unions cannot be foretold easily on complex issues in economic policy, e.g, employment policy, price policy, energy policy, and liberties. Insofar as such people are trained in social analysis, insofar as they have differing views as to the Good pertinent to the given situation, insofar as they can look ahead to discern implications that the uninitiated cannot see, the views of the sophisticates will differ from the knee jerk reactions of the ideologues. But sophisticates and experts will also differ from each other. Thus in the preparation of legislation or administrative regulation there will be protagonists for and antagonists against a given position. But there will also be a vast number of views on details, views which the major protagonists and antagonists will overlook or even not care about.

Ideals or ideology, as well as technical competence, play roles in attitude creation. Even in objective, technical analysis there persists a thread of value preference, a thread which cannot be eliminated. Traditional economists are rarely political radicals, or radicals in any other social movement. To be sure, there are exceptions, but as a general matter the discipline of economics attracts those who have a respect for a certain kind of order. A long academic experience influences sociologists to be more accepting of planned social changes, an attribute which seems to offend many businessmen. Marxian economists, with very rare exceptions, are on the political left, and also tend to be critical of other than economic institutions. A kind of hidden agenda is carried around in the back of the minds of even impartial experts. Milton Friedman, who claims to be objective in his analysis, is clearly one of the Western world's leading latter day moralists.

At bottom, however, the political left and right in the United States (and western Europe) hold to more or less common basic values or value conceptions related to the goodness of income (if not to its distribution). But they differ in their analyses of other values. Such differences may lead to different policies and programs, and thereby to different intermediate goals. Each of the many pressure groups clothes itself in the mantle of morality and justice.[8]

It is as if morality is what one wants done to others, and justice is what one wants done to him. The "I" and "thou" dialogue is essential in lawmaking, for laws are compromises among moral, technical, and generous components. And each group, indeed each person, hopes the result is justice to its members and to him personally. This is said in neither criticism nor jest. Compromise is the essence of lawmaking. In the United States (and probably in the Soviet Union as well) regulation and law are fortunately not the pure, clean products of ideologues. Such single minded people are boring, dangerous, and, on the whole, social liabilities. Avoidance of conflict is a great social value.

The tariff issue once was a great one in American life. Among first year graduate students in economics the issue persisted until recent times. The late Frank Knight of the University of Chicago used to announce that if economics teaches us anything, it teaches that the world's income is lowered by the imposition of tariffs. But not all the world had the opportunity to study with Knight, *nor are the only issues that concern people and governments the world's income.* Other issues, economic and noneconomic, intrude. Therefore the conclusion that morality would be served by cutting tariffs to zero, and at once, is irrelevant and probably wrong. A program of adjustments and gradual tariff reduction, which gives a great opportunity for small and large pressures to be applied, may make sense. The goals other than the world's income, e.g., employment in Detroit or Manchester, or short range pressing problems of balance of payments, or subsidy policies to exports, must be considered and handled. The wisest course, realistically speaking, as contrasted to a very simple model of foreign trade, is obviously not to cut tariffs immediately and unilaterally. Compromise among the affected, accomplished by persuasion, is a more meaningful model of behavior than a rigid, determinate model which seeks to maximize some abstract function. Morality and justice are not and cannot be achieved by the mechanical approach. There is always more in Heaven and on earth than in one's philosophy.

Regulation and law are the products of compromise and pressure, but the basic ideological deep down drives tend to be fairly widespread in society. So regulation and law are not often viscously self-contradictory. The very act of compromising in making policy becomes an integral part of the Good, of the ideal of society. For the recognition of other interests and other points of view makes life tolerable and society more stable. The act of compromising is a species of generosity. An interest group might have the power to force its point of view into a law or regulation. The implications are disobedience, social unrest, and coalitions against the pressuring group. These are not stabilizing factors. Compromise, by not fully exploiting power, social, political, or economic, converts it to a social force, for not fully using power is to enhance the relative power of other groups.

Economic or business interests are obviously very important insofar as they affect the social income and its distribution. But it is difficult for businessmen and spokesmen for business institutions to understand that noneconomic and nonbusiness forces play increasingly greater roles as the levels of national and personal income rise. It is also difficult for such persons to recognize that income is not the only economic measure of social stability and success. Employment, price levels, quality of output, distribution of income and wealth, various economic and business quantities which businessmen consider as means, are ends to great fractions, indeed the majority, of the population.

Justice to the business man, what he gets out of the system, what is done to him, is important—to both him and everyone else. For if businessmen as a class feel unjustified, the entire society will suffer. But the business community perforce has to be concerned with morality, with what is done to and for other groups and individuals, in the light of *their* values. For what appears to the business fraternity as a matter of morality, is a matter of justice to everyone else.

We have devised guidelines for the content of the ethics of business. We know where we should be going, in a general way, but not the detail of the trip. The specifics are unknown, and unknowable in advance. Social as well as individual life is a progression of events, but we are ignorant of whether they are determined or not. The practical conclusion is that we, as individuals and as groups, should act *as if* we do have something to contribute, and so have a role in determining the future. Experience has overwhelmingly proved to each of us that we have neither complete control nor foreknowledge of the events of our lives. Only the most exasperating ideologue can prate that the world's future is determined and he knows what it is going to be. We have neither the time nor inclination to consider seriously such categorical nonsense.

The world, and any of its segments, must be assumed to be ordered in some fashion—that is, to follow some rules of change, which however are not uniquely set—otherwise analysis is impossible. Alternative orders and behaviors are assumed by all who try to analyze. Furthermore, unknown factors impinge on the system. They are the elements from outside the system in question, or are unknown because of unavoidable ignorance. An advertising program for tourism to Greece, a program which seems foolproof, can fall to nothing because of a cholera scare in Yugoslavia, or a threat of Middle East war, or the adverse balance of payments of the United States. Such events have come to pass in the past decade. No business firm can be expected either to know about or be able to control a cholera threat six months in advance. No firm can control United States foreign purchases, nor solve the Israeli–Arab–Soviet Union–U.S. political imbalances. So our attempt to discover the relevant implications for planned or considered action is never likely to be complete. But not all issues are so complex or far-reaching as some of the examples we have adduced. Questions of minimum wage, energy, welfare, education, tariff policies are much more amenable to analysis and moral evaluation at the Grand Ethic level than are the alarums and excursions which confuse the orderliness of life.

When business deals with individuals or small entities, in general it may be assumed that power—economic and analytic power—is on the side of business. Given the uncertainties and complexities of life for all, given the superiority of business in any transaction we are envisioning, we suggest that the moral, ethical basis of business behavior is generosity and compromise, and adherence to law and convention. Giving a little more than law or convention requires is generosity, if constrained by the analysis of implication. To be sure, this does not mean giving the store away or ruining the business to be a good guy. But it does mean that acting in the interests of others is moral, if the action is in the direction suggested by the value system, and the integrity of the firm is not in question.

The counterweight to this is in policy making at the grand level. Here where law and regulation are being devised, social stability and generally accepted social goals must be considered by all contending parties. Power is then tempered by the value system, and adjustments are made, again after examining as best one can the implications of the available alternatives. In business, as in military tactics and strategy, one tends to doubt a line of action which promises complete success for one's forces and chaos for the enemy. Rarely are such complete goals feasible. Where timidity ends and realism begins, and where realism ends and blind faith begins, are not easy to mark out. But the Middle Way is an ideal. This means tempering power with restraint.

In the middle market level of business decisions, we suggest that the rules of the market, in general, should be adhered to. First, the legal requirements here are stringent. This involves justice as the operation of law. But second, and of equal importance, to diverge from the legal and market convention often requires adjustments. But the firm, in the market, is not making public policy and has no license to do so. Therefore the firm should be obedient to the higher authority of the law. Generosity is still available. But exploitation by power is disruptive of the whole system of policy making in a democracy. And the economic game is played by legal rules, not by changing market rules as one goes along. In the latter direction lie instability and even chaos.

7

WHAT TO DO UNTO OTHERS?

The most commonly accepted rule used in America as the ethical structure, the conceptual system, is the Golden Rule—"Do unto others as you would have others do unto you." Stated slightly more rigorously, it is "Act so that each of your acts may become a universal law."

This revered principle of behavior places great weight on the doer of deeds. On him, if he follows the rule, is placed the burden of determining the ethical content of his act. The doee, the one who is acted on, is without voice or vote. Yet the recipient of the action, the doee, is the person most affected by the act. The story of the radical speaker in Union Square comes to mind. "After the revolution," he intones, "workers will eat strawberries and cream, just like the bosses." "But," objects a mild fellow in the audience, "I don't like strawberries and cream." The speaker is irate and shouts "Comes the revolution you'll eat strawberries and cream and like it."

Most questions of active people are not concerned with morality or ethics. Active men and women face tasks of varying degrees of difficulty which require both skill and habit, as well as ingenuity. In the ordinary course of life the important perplexing problems are often technical and organizational. The fruitful life of the late twentieth century is not the ideal life of the moral philosophor nor the idealized life of the God-intoxicated man or woman of the pre-Enlightenment era. Morality exists for those who have other things to do than merely being moral.[1]

But, and there always is the "but," morality, justice, and ethics, the elements which legitimate our actions, demand our thought. Morality and justice are what join and separate us, what legitimate our behavior and in large part define the several societies in which we live.

The issues of legitimation—justice for individuals, morality as conformance to accepted modes of behavior, ethics as the joining of justice and morality—are of universal interest, although their content is not universally identical. Problems of ethical significance lead to the question of how well a society with its particular events performs its functions within the confines of an accepted value system. The value system defines the norms of behavior. It is departures from the norms which generate considerations of good and bad, legitimated or non-legitimated behavior.

The world is a play of people. The environment is the setting. Insofar as the environment is physical, it may be analyzed and explained by the sciences. Insofar as the environment is more ephemeral—that is, spiritual, psychological, or social—it may be analyzed by the social disciplines. The analysis, in the latter case, is usually less clean cut and satisfying than physical analyses.

The social environment is largely a given for the individual or the firm. To some extent powerful persons, powerful in their ingenuity, skill, wealth, or wisdom, may influence their environments but rarely dramatically. Markets, our major concern, are not made by sellers, although they can be influenced by sellers. The salesman who tries to sell refrigerators to Eskimos in January has at best a spotty sales record. But an automobile company can do well in a geographically extended society which is willing to spend public money on roads. Or a drug company can do well if it creates the illusion of good looks, vigor, youth, and sex appeal, or even of only reducing pain and ennui, all for a modest price!

The values which people, as individuals, develop are reflections of social values. Such values grow over time by action. Some are neglected or cast out; for example, the extended family does not have the moral value in the United States that it had seventy-five to one hundred years ago. The Social Security Act of F.D.R., in part, was a recognition of changing family values, and in part a positive reaction to a growing social desire for limiting family responsibility. The result was a strengthened ideology regarding the independence, or greater independence, of the nuclear family. This in turn led to other legislation, insurance sales, and novel social attitudes. Events both are made by man and make man.²

An economic or a business system is justified or legitimated by how well it performs. Performance, however, is not merely economic. That goods and services must be produced in sufficient quantities, and of sufficient quality, to satisfy users is of course essential. But business has a greater task than allocating resources most effectively and distributing income in accordance with some model which assumes income maximization. Business has a greater task, in brief, than merely requiring each firm to act competitively so that the whole system produces a maximum income at a minimal cost.

Adam Smith's invisible hand lacks strength and cunning. It is generally agreed that the Department of Justice and Federal Trade Commission bring legal actions against a very small percentage of firms which, in fact, exercise market power beyond the limits of competition. But even if the invisible hand were omnipotent in a market situation, it would not guarantee the satisfactory completion of all the tasks business is given in the ongoing world.

For one thing, equity and justice must be assured, if only approximately. Justice and equity are not natural in the sense of being in nature. They are personal expectations based on complex notions of fairness, need, self-evaluation, and custom or convention.

Second, morality and social acceptability must be roughly achieved. These too, are not fixed ideas, but vary with circumstances and the nature of the activity being considered. The market cannot be relied on to assure, for example, the quality of food, drugs, or even tires. But then neither can the government agencies. Here is a dilemma. It will, I should guess, not be resolved simply by putting greater reliance on markets and less on regulation.

Third, the joining in time and place of justice and morality, of the personal and the social, suggest an ethical action. But this is not enough. If a business or a person merely satisfies the social requirements in the treatment of a person, in adherence to law or convention, the action is clearly not bad. But is it good? Obedience to law is expected, but usually it does not win an award. To be good, that is to engage in an act which we may call ethical, one has to go beyond the usual. One has to give a person more than his due, and behave beyond the requirements of custom. This is what I meant when I asserted that active, busy people are not primarily, nor even usually, concerned with morality or ethics.

Ethical behavior is nothing if it is not freely willed. Thus such behavior being operative in the future implies thought—synthetic thought. The immediate participants in an action, in our case a business transaction, are not always the only ones involved. In economics we have a wonderful notion called "externalities" or "market failure." A transaction or an action may affect those not parties to the transaction or who have no immediate stake in the action. A firm contracts to buy sulfurous coal, which is a kind of brimstone, and burns it. It is cheaper than alternative fuels; it tends to minimize costs. But only the firm's costs. Other firms and householders suffer and are put to all sorts of expenses to offset the hellish nuisance. The market simply has failed to assure the welfare of the neighborhood. Or, as another example with which the late twentieth century is replete, a firm in good faith produces and markets a drug which, it turns out, causes more damage than cure. Again the market has failed.

But not all market failures are bad. Firms train labor, which finds employment in other, even competing firms. This, on the net, is good because the skill of labor has been improved, and the training firm itself has the chance of hiring persons trained by competitors. Or a firm develops a printing process which reproduces color more accurately than any other process. As a result, paintings and other works of art can be reproduced in color for the joy and enlightenment of all who love art. The benefits, by any rational, social accounting, are far in excess of the profits the firm enjoys, or the profits of the firm plus the losses of its competitors, assuming they cannot get hold of the new process or something like it.

Given the significant role of externalities—that is, the nonmarket effects of a business action or transaction—it becomes obvious that ethical considerations cannot be limited to the immediate participants. Contracts and invisible hands are not enough to assure that business is oriented toward at least ethically neutral behavior. Nor can contracts and invisible hands assume that behavior is directed toward, or even not away from, ethical behavior. Competition by itself does not assure morality.

Cooperation among firms immediately comes to mind as a way to get at moral results. But a moment's reflection makes one doubt that cooperation, broadly concerned, is likely to generate acceptable solutions in particular cases.

The lion and the lamb may lie down in a spirit of cooperative conciliation, but only the lion is likely to arise, and a less hungry lion. Cooperation, joint action, of course has its place in social intercourse. Lack of cooperation with respect to the rules and laws of running a city results in most of the evils and uglinesses of large cities. The opposite of cooperation may be seen as selfishness—that is, lack of loyalty to the rights or needs of others.

For a big business, or indeed for any business, to determine by itself the rules and conventions business should follow, or for a political executive, regardless of rank, to make such rules, is to injure the democratic spirit. Rules and laws are the province of legislatures; and presumably such bodies are more aware of, and responsive to, the variety of public opinions and ideologies than a business manager or even the president of the United States.

But once rules and conventions are arrived at, often by elaborate compromises, they more often than not require discretion in their application. Discretion by managers and by public administrators, including the judiciary, is a necessity in most circumstances.

Discretion requires not merely the softening of a rule to give consideration to "good faith" undertakings which are in the process of being adjusted, or to give more leeway to market forces. Discretion by judge or manager also requires a concern for the implications of the considered behavior. In a real sense, all such discretion implies a concern for externalities. Particular behavior may spread over the social system in strange and wondrous ways.

The aura or environment which bathes a given action, once the action is legitimated, may be applied to other, less desirable action, creating a false environment of legitimation. It is well known that if the leading personality of a business institution is known to accept graft or to bend the rules for his own purposes, others in the business will try to get away with the same sort of behavior. The legitimation has to do with the justice of equal treatment of and benefits for both goose and gander.

In addition, an action by a firm may, in the first instance, be justifiable; but an extension which flows from the action may not be desirable. Industries which use whale oil, or societies which use whale meat, benefit from whaling. But the social loss of whales, as a species strikes other people as decidedly contrary to ideological values which are relevant. So conflict results.

The implications of behavior, environmental, economic, and ideological, are of great importance to the functioning of the social world. So long as Big Business, Big Labor, Big Government, Big Science, Big Charity, Big Almost Everything Else except consuming households dominate the social world, the implications of behavior by big institutions are far reaching and powerful. On such implications depend the environment of justice and morality.[3]

Novelty and legitimation in the morality and justice environments are created often by opinion makers and leaders, news media, artists, schools, colleges, religious organizations, and so on. However, by a process which is not clear, more ordinary people too (probably classifiable by wealth, education, geographic location, and background) seem to create and communicate ideological strands which may become quite powerful. The anti-Vietnam War attitude of the 1960s, the Anti-Trust attitude of the late nineteenth century, the current attitudes toward sex and the family, each have their apologists. The acceptance of values by such apologists, often quite ordinary folk, is necessary to legitimate attitudes which are novel and growing, without much reference to accepted doctrine.

To ascertain what a course of business action implies for those not immediately affected requires analysis. The analysis generally employed is economics and its derivatives, e.g., marketing, finance, operations research and statistical forecasting. The methodological base or ideal of such analytic efforts tends to derive from the successful hard sciences. The methodology of sciences such as physics, the ideal type, combines logic and empiricism. No one expects pure symbolic logic or mathematics, by itself, to prognosticate the future of a physical universe. Empiricism is here to stay. Instrumentation has become a great tool of science. Physical and chemical analyses which require complex statistical and quantitative manipulation benefit from the engineering ingenuity of modern research technology.

New ideas, however, are harder to come by. The invention of new conceptual ways of looking at the world is very difficult.

But our concern is with the social disciplines, primarily business. The success of physics in the recent past has externalized itself in the business sciences. Technique, usually mathematical, with an almost universal reliance on the computer, has captured the imagination of ambitious journal editors and academics, researchers under the age of forty, and students, especially the better students. Even though the math and statistics are inveighed against by students, the measure of their accomplishment, especially at the graduate level, is much greater than it was a generation ago. But data, no matter how elegantly manipulated (students say massaged and manicured), are no better than they are.

It is clear that data on such matters as prices and quantities, or employment and unemployment, data of extreme importance, as collected, are not like the data which the texts and models require if their analyses are to be followed. To comment on two kinds of numbers—prices and unemployment—is to expose the imperfections. Prices and unemployment in the "real world" are generated or constructed by forces which are not included in any static or persistent static conceptual definition, if for no other reason than that random and exogenous forces are among those which determine prices and unemployment.

This indeterminacy problem may also exist outside business analysis, but that does not justify treating prices and/or unemployment as if they were each uniquely determined. These damnable random and exogenous variables are serpents in the Garden of Order, or the unknown unknowables which make analysis and prognostication so difficult. And what has no place in the argument is exactly what is of major importance in an ethical evaluation, namely the values expressed by the ideas of justice, morality and ethics.

A business firm being evaluated for its behavior should be analyzed in relation to (1) its setting or environment, which is largely a market consideration, (2) its internal structure, and (3) its goals and resources. Except for the questions related to the setting or environment, these three approaches are no different from those an investor would use to analyze a company. The first consideration, however, is traditional only if environment is taken to include market situation and legally or conventionally delimited externalities, e.g., smoke abatement or medical care for employees. A social, moral, or value oriented investigation would include such elements as the immediate external effects of the firm's behavior on the market, on the nonmarket environment (or on people in and outside the firm), and finally on the more general environment.

The ultimate evaluation of business, as we see it, is the weighing of the economic benefit against the ethical implications, the latter with particular reference to people as individuals. This may sound eminently sensible, but among many, perhaps the majority of, economists the evaluation of business as to its goodness is limited to the adherence to certain structural and legal criteria. That the firm is not the keeper of society's conscience is a proposition of great merit. But this should not be taken to mean that the firm, personalized as the manager, may not engage in actions which go beyond those prescribed by law and custom. If his employers, for whom he is the surrogate, disapprove of the manager's behavior they may dismiss him. The major question, it would appear, is to what degree or in what fashion a manager may depart from legal requirements or conventional constraints. Certainly not in the direction of acting as if his firm or an association of firms might set the rules without reference to constituted authorities. We have agencies whose social function it is to set law and rule, after compromises have been worked out. We cannot see ethical behavior stemming from joint, combinational behavior among firms in the same market except under circumstances too unusual to be considered here. Nor can we see managerial behavior which is illegal being justified, again except under most rare conditions. Obedience to law and convention, a concern with assisting in the adjustment of law and convention, these seem to be the major requirements of a firm. And yet, we suggest, such less-than-bold behavior does not lead to ethical ends. The firm, as we see it, is in most market situations not much of an ethical instrument, nor should it be if legislation and public administration are to be such instruments. In personal and lesser personnel matters, which are really subordinate to the implications of market behavior, questions of ethical behavior are more likely to be involved.

Business, as a social institution, is not analogous to a machine, but neither is it analogous to a family or society. Business is part of society, and therefore constrained by the ideological constraints we associate in the United States with democracy and individualism. Business is not *a* democracy, it is part of *the* democracy.

The freedom of business to act is limited by law and convention. It is also limited by its technical and capital structure, financial resources, knowledge, and market and political power. Briefly the several environments of the firm limit and even direct its behavior.[4] The particulars of these elements differ with changing attitudes and values over time.

Thus the ethical evaluation of business behavior is always in relation to the setting of business. A firm about to go bankrupt, which steals or otherwise illegally and improperly acquires some needed money, cannot ethically justify its behavior on the grounds that to do otherwise would have meant its demise. Its circumstance cannot justify its actions. On the other side, a firm which knowingly breaks the law by its trading practices to help the salesman of the Northern Ireland "cause" in 1979, or the Spanish Republic "cause" in 1936, may make a claim for ethical and moral justification. The claim may not be justified if one generalizes the argument to allow a firm to set the foreign policy of the nation.

The ethics of business behavior is not determined or judged by how business evaluates its behavior in the light of the alternate opportunities open to it. Generally speaking, the effects of normal market behavior are less dramatic than those we hypothesized above. Economic effects (price-quality), aesthetic effects, personal and personnel effects, general market and general social effects, are the categories which come to mind. These are available for consideration by the manager. How he considers such effects, and the skill with which he evaluates them determine his managerial status and quality. But the more meaningful evaluations are made by others, by people outside the firm. For this purpose, shareholders are outside the firm. The outsiders, the observers, use the yardsticks of (1) justice as concerned with effects on people, (2) morality as concerned with social implications, and (3) ethics, the two combined in accordance with the mores of time and place. (1) and (2) above are not synonymous, nor is (2) merely the sum of the individuals of (1). Justice, as we delimit it, adheres to individuals, whilst morality is a function of group values. Some degree of social organization is necessary for a moral climate to evince itself. To be sure an individual's notion of justice arises from his experience and expectations, but the incidence is personal. The distinction between personnel and industrial relations is, perhaps, analogous. In business usage generally, the former deals with the placement, testing, and promotion of persons as individuals. The latter deals with the relations between management as an institution, and the work force organized into a union, or as an organic body, if the plant is not unionized.

Justice, morality, and ethics are not arrived at by analysis alone. Analysis is necessary to winnow out the elements which make up a person's "due," or a society's "bundle of ideologies." As evaluations, however, justice and morality are measures of behavior and reaction to behavior. It is one thing to ask if an act completed in the past was ethical. It is quite another thing to ask if an action not undertaken, and hence all its conditions not known, would be ethical. The memory of events and their evaluation in the future constitute the work of imagination. The capacity to imagine a setting and place in it a behavior, then estimate the moral nature of an action in terms of its outreach in space and time, is no small task. Techniques of forecasting come into play, but all who have tried social forecasting know how imperfect it is. Yet there are some people who intuitively (for want of a better word) are able to guess future implications better than others. Such synthesizers are rare in management, and among the observers outside management. Everyone, or nearly everyone, plays at being judge of the future because we all desire to know what the implications of behavior, our own and others', will be.

In general, we feel secure and comforted if we have some general rules to guide us in business, in our professional and personal lives. Such comfort, however, is frequently found to be short lived as we bump into the reality of particulars. Not everyone who feels secure is secure. But no one who does not feel secure is secure. Experience is often an effective destroyer of the security blanket, as well as a provider of the self-assurance that experience so often brings. Decision making in business (or elsewhere) always takes place under conditions of uncertainty. Indeed if one were certain, his decision would be automatic. Uncertainty grows with the complexity of the task's setting, is part of the task, and is always implied in futurity.

The ethically oriented businessman, then, trying to gauge the effects of his behavior, needs a rule, or at least would benefit from one. "Do unto others as you would have them do unto you" has a long history as a vague piece of ethical advice. I submit it is meaningless at best, dangerous at worst. Let us examine its worth.

Armed with this rule, our manager faces the future. He is also armed with a memory—that is, with how his world worked in the past—and with a model of the particular exercise he wants to undertake. He also has a model of how the world is likely to act in the future, and how the future will react to the action he is about to inject into it. The constraint he sets himself is that the people who will be affected by his action will enjoy (or suffer) results that he, the manager, would characterize as just were the same results imposed on him. You will note in all this that the wishes, desires, hopes, and feelings of justice of the *affected* are given no weight. The action is viewed as a personal, not a social or moral phenomenon, albeit it has social effects.

What if the manager has a streak of sado-masochism in him? What if the recipients of the manager's actions are unlike him in age, outlook, and ideologies? What if the subjects of his actions are confirmed anchorites? or Hispanics while he is an Anglo? One can continue in this line to show that value systems are not common in their entirety throughout a society. One can also recognize the moral uniqueness and rigidity implied by a "Do Unto Others" rule.

Too often we assume that people in general, or at least "nice people," are endowed with a common set of values and ethics; or what is equally wrong, that conceptions of ethics are fixed in a given society. It seems rather that there is a bundle of ideologies in a society, and different circumstances call up different handfuls of values, for ideologies are values in action. Nature has not endowed anyone with a system of values; society provides them.[5] But it is remarkable that some rare people can invent and instill values in society. Sometimes such rare people are called charismatic, sometimes spiritual or political leaders. How it happens is beyond my knowledge, but not beyond my experience. Hitler, Roosevelt, and Mao, in politics, have recently had this capacity. Exotic spiritual leaders from the Orient have bemused or enthralled many young Americans, even in current times. In art, too, there are figures who, unconsciously perhaps, impose their ideals on artists.

But in business the spiritual seems lacking. No matter how big companies advertise their products' virtues, or the virtues of business as an institution, the cries seem awkward, flat, and false. We all know that there is a catch, even a Catch 22, hidden somewhere in the rhetoric.

I think that the claim of business that the business society and community is a great one, or that American society is great because business made it so, or that one should support free enterprise because free enterprise supports us, sounds a little ridiculous and very pompous. The advertisements are cast in terms of generalizations and generalities. But to say that business is just great permits us to test the generalization. Who has not bought a lemon of a car, television, or house? Immediate memory and experience show the assertion to be false, as a generalization.

On the other hand, who has not been intrigued by some advertisements where a particular is stressed? A particular which stands on its own and does not wrap itself in the flag or suggest impossible externalities. We want our mail order hats or low calorie foods to be specifically hats and food. A particular which laughs at us and at itself is also a good advertising gimmick. Truth, justice, and morality are not issues we want to hear about in a puff for a product.

To follow a general rule in an uncertain future, to follow a general rule without regard to the interests of those affected, even though the rule be one of ethics, to follow a general rule when particularity is involved, is to risk unethical behavior. Perhaps the safe rule for business, a rule which cannot be rigorously adhered to, would be "Do unto others as they would be done unto."

8

DOING THINGS RIGHT IS NOT ALWAYS DOING THE RIGHT THING

Competence is more important than the purpose of the organization for many people who work. They become obsessed with doing things right, rather than worry about doing the right things. The movie *Bridge over the River Kwai* stated this dilemma in crystal clear form. A company of British engineers were prisoners of the Japanese in Asia. When forced to build a difficult bridge over a troublesome chasm, they performed superbly and professionally amid harrowing experiences. The only problem was that in so doing they were aiding the enemy to victory over their own country. It was only after commandos had blown the structure to bits that the imprisoned commander asked himself, "What have I done?" The possibility of treason never occurred to him during the daily drill of performing an admittedly marvellous feat of engineering.

An ethical system, like any other social system, is an artifact. It is a mental conception of the values implicit in the motives, constraints, goals, and efforts of an enterprise. The observer looking at a set of alternative behaviors puts them into some sort of hierarchical value order in his mind. It is not very meaningful to ask whether such order exists in *reality* in nature. That the observer sees the behavior is orderly is sufficient. Reality to another observer may be something else. Whichever system of explanation needs fewer assumptions, predicts and explains better, is the efficient, economic one. The acceptance or rejection of the order depends on how well it may be used to explain what happens. This is a pragmatic or operational approach.[1]

Such questions as "Is there a business ethic?" or "Should there be a business ethic?" are, in my opinion, not very good questions. Social institutions, and business is such an institution, *require* social acceptance for their continuance.[2] Business exists because it provides services which are wanted and beneficial. If alternative institutions can provide the wanted outputs and services, such institutions are candidates to replace the existing business institution. Evaluations of institutions tend to follow three lines of attack: (1) defense of the status quo, (2) reform, or (3) replacement by another set of institutions. Evaluation of the business institution has these three camps. The status quo camp is very small. The replacement camp seems to lack thoughtfulness, at least to this writer. The reform camp is composed of a myriad of confusing and conflicting ideas; but this camp seems to hold the seeds of the future.

The number of youngsters who, after the 1960s, opted for the "good life" on the little-mechanized farm or in the commune is minuscule. Even those dropouts relied on the market—that is, on business—for both purchase and sale. At most, those who withdrew were critical of some supposedly dehumanizing aspects of business life. But business, as busy-ness, is a psychological as well as a social necessity to maintain a population in some sort of meaningful order. Business helps keep people out of mischief! This is not an unimportant function.

At an informal dinner early in the Carter administration, when the more insightful of the population were recognizing the significance of the energy problems of the nation and their relation to inflation, I heard a physician excoriate business. Two businessmen attending the dinner had just returned from New York, where they had gone, attracted by an advertisement in the ubiquitous *New York Times,* for Cadillacs. The ad seems to have suggested that, with cash, one might buy a grand car for $4,000 less than anywhere else. The two friends made the trip, found the ad a come-on (as successful businessmen they should have known this, since no dealer gives autos away below market prices and advertises it). However the two friends did strike deals better than they might have made at home, and each was the owner of a brand new 14-mpg car, with many gadgets and much status.

Our medical friend listened to the story of the trip, and then exploded. No one, he averred, no businessman, could *honestly* get together $16,000 or $20,000 in cash, at a moment's notice, and no one

with a shred of honor and social concern would buy a gas guzzler
when the very stability of the republic required modesty and restraint.
Indeed he himself was driving a (large and elegant, I add) VW.

The two business types were dumbfounded by the attack, which
they considered quite personal. Their responses were different, however. One tried to calm his irate medical friend and accuser by suggesting that life is like that, and after all how much gasoline would
he use in a year, or even a decade for that matter? The other's defense was more spirited. This merchant argued that he did not spend
much money on himself, he rarely drank, and never ran around spend-
ing his fortune. The car was his joy and necessity. Besides, and this
was the clincher, he did not live on so grand a scale as physicians,
by which he meant the medico at hand, and if oil was scarce *why in
hell didn't Congress or Carter or someone do something about it?*
The sharpness was blunted by the usual change in dinner conversations.

Later, the next day, I raised the question of the ethics of car buying with the three men separately. Each felt, upon reflection, that
indeed a grave ethical question of behavior had been raised. But the
conception of the ethical issues were quite different for the three men.

The physician's view was centered on the behavior of business and
businessmen. He had for the past several years been chairman of the
radiological department of his teaching hospital. He had traveled over
the United States and Europe, dealing with firms whose sales to this
single hospital might have amounted to $3 or $3.5 million. Our physician was first taken in, later horrified, by the expensive treatment accorded him, and by the hints of the offers and counter offers of the
sellers to him. Furthermore the physician seemed to have guilt feelings about his own financial success. Finally he felt that the government's present policy of restricting radiological "scanners" was stupid
and counterproductive. Wherever he looked, he saw little people seeking their own petty interests, and despite Adam Smith's supposed
constraint, there was no Invisible Hand which ultimately secured the
best for the most. While our medical friend had no solution, he did
feel that if only people were "honest and sincere" the world would
get on better.

The first businessman, a successful building contractor, saw the
ethical issue as related to power. Individuals and groups (e.g., trade

associations, trade unions, political administrations) with power, got their way, roughly in proportion to their power, which was not defined. Power seemed to be, in his mind, the capacity to force someone else to act by withholding something, e.g., going on strike or refusing to let a contract. For him the villain in the auto story was the retailer who administered with duplicity and then tried to take the buyer in. He was not outraged, but he resented being put in the position of a patsy to a dealer in New York, because the local Cadillac dealer (a friend of his) also lost, by not selling two cars he otherwise would have sold, and at high prices.

The second businessman, who was engaged in managing a large personal service activity, had two feelings. The physician, an old friend, should not have accused him of getting income improperly. As a business manager he always did what was expected of him for the good of the business and its employees. He felt no shame on that score.

On the bigger issue, he felt that he did not make the laws, he obeyed and interpreted them. If energy was an issue, there are people and institutions paid to handle such issues. It was not his job, and if everyone acted to make policy, the world would be in a mess. He felt that public issues, e.g., unemployment, inflation, military policies, were his concern only insofar as he voted and paid taxes. His major worries were for his firm, his employees, and the owners.

What was common among the three was the ultimate belief that goodness must be done, that morality and justice are essential. But the content of the three beliefs, the ways of administering, assuring, and assigning them, were divergent to the point of being almost unrelated.

All agree that the business world is not an ethical delight, but all agree that an approach toward an ethical system is infinitely more desirable than departure from the ethic. Ethics is behavior.

Behavior, in our society, indeed in any society, requires an ultimate justification. Behavior, individual or social, which affects no one other than the actor is rare. The concept of victimless crime, e.g., prostitution, is an interesting one only if it is not pushed very far. Some hold that prostitution is inherently wicked, others that it spreads "social" diseases, others hold that it is degrading to the prostitute. All these and similar arguments state that, in the mind of the particular speaker, prostitution is not in accord with ethics as he sees it. Prostitution therefore is not legitimated, and so fails the ultimate test of acceptability. In spite of the folk belief that prostitution is inherently profitable for its managers, its very profitability is probably related to the reluctance of many investors in capital, labor, and land to enter that market. Its success is a success of scarcity, and its scarcity is a reflection of its lack of social acceptability.

In society, for better or worse, each person is forced to consider himself to some degree his brother's and sister's keeper. The ethical system of our society is not an empty, formal, set of ideas that has no reality except in conversation; it is a set of values in action. The set may be for some systematized, or for others may consist of a set of discrete propositions. But it is operative. One may not like it, but there it is.

To one person a firm has an obligation to lay off workers if profits are negative or low. To another person the firm, under similar circumstances, has an obligation to maintain employment, at least on a part time basis, especially if unemployment is rife and jobs are hard to come by. To one person oil and gas prices should rise to induce firms to search for oil. To another oil firms should not be permitted to make profits from the national shortage of energy. It is clear that the content of an ethic depends on the social conventions, ideology, law, analytic capacity, and utopian ideals of the society and the institutional managers. People differ with respect to their sensitivity to and interpretation of such considerations. Therefore, as one should expect, there are differences in ethical outlooks and evaluations.

Can we nevertheless suggest any basis for a guide which would unite purely business purposes to an ethical bond or justification? A guide to a manager's choices (both economic and ethical), we suggest, is to be found in a doctrine of implication. This doctrine holds that any action which a manager directs, and the firm undertakes, should be valued in terms of further effects of the action, not only within the firm but generally. The idea is obvious, but often neglected. It is the idea of planning, of management by objective, of budgeting and cost effectiveness, of "Look ahead! In your mind take two or three steps before you take one actual one." It is the antithesis of instant gratification.

Virtually everyone would agree that there are certain rules or constraints that all must obey if society of any sort is to get on with its tasks, let alone flourish. In business a certain degree of trustworthiness without a written contract, a conception of mutuality and sharing, but not including conspiracy, and a willingness and capacity to operate within certain unwritten rules or codes of behavior are all necessary. It is when these are breached or thought to be breached that the ethical questions have to be faced, unless, in a dynamic business circumstance, a sudden change or requirement alters the situation. Then conventional, even legally sanctioned, behavior may undergo great changes, and new norms will be sought. To the degree that the business world is dynamic and adjustive, such new norms are necessary concomitants. Old rules may be reinterpreted as new guides, and brand new rules may be invented. The "point system" in mortgage loans, by which special fees were required by banks extending mortgages, was a way around legal maximum interest rates when market rates were very high. The practice of some firms to classify employees as salaried, managerial personnel is sometimes a way around legally required overtime payments for hourly workers. The abrogation of contracts in an inflation, and the invention of indexing are attempts to make impossible situations workable. In a dynamic, intrarelated world the results of actions flow in many directions.

On a happier note, firms requiring high level technical proficiency from suppliers, I learned from a study I did for the Small Business Administration, sometimes assist their suppliers in solving the production problems of *other buyers!*[3] The favors, of course, are often returned, but not on any contractual base. Routinely firms train employees who, after a time, leave for jobs in other firms, carrying with them their acquired skills. Yet this has not led firms with expensive training programs continually to hoard their labor force (as was the case under the old apprenticeship and craftsmen systems). Indeed the laws limiting specific performance recognize the private ownership of a skill or knowledge, however secured.

Applied to the area of ethics, the doctrine of implication suggests that the manager try to imagine, or get his staff to analyze, the probable effects of his firm's behavior on those who are positioned both close to and away from the center of the action. Then the manager can even suggest to those who might be affected what might be in store for them. It is even possible that new, alternative modes of behavior will be countersuggested, or thought up, if the distant effects are onerous. We are suggesting that externalities be thought through and, being out of the immediate business and economic spheres, be valued in the ethical sphere.[4]

The ethical requirement here is one of notice and warning, and possibly of alternative action. The doctrine does not provide a guide to what should be done under specific circumstances. Rather, it suggests a way of behaving in general, a philosophy or vision of the firm as related to other social entities. It does not stress problem solving (as an ethical matter) so much as it stresses problem avoidance for those who may be adversely affected.[5]

The doctrine of implication is not always adhered to by management, and indeed has been abused. A manager whose firm has the reputation for dynamic change lets it be known that a change of great significance is imminent. Plans to rearrange the labor force are openly discussed, buyers are alerted, indeed a whole line of action is hinted at, with the major purpose being, actually, to keep buyers from considering the purchase of a competitor's line. That such a policy has been followed by at least one of *Fortune*'s 500 is a fact, certified by legal decree. Trying to control a market by false statements is clearly an abuse according to the doctrine of implication. Another case of abuse, or at least disregard, is the case of a drug company's selling a product which benefited patients but harmed their then unborn offspring! In these cases the implications of the firm's behavior was known, or at least knowable with little effort.

A less sordid weakness is that the investigation of implication is often costly and uncertain. Who knows, in advance, whether a process will work, or how it will work in all details? The drug company referred to did not plan to harm the unborn, nor was anyone then certain that the effects would be felt in the second generation. Scientific warnings were at hand. Unheeded warning or advice might make the manager out to be evil at worst, or incompetent at best.

But more significant is the difficulty, costliness, and technical limitation of analyzing an imagined change. The warning to the manager may have been less than persuasive and convincing. And there is no way to recover such analytical costs except to include them as capital costs, which might reduce the chance of a new product or process from making the grade. Knowledge and the best will in the world often are simply inadequate to cope with future problems which are ill defined. Reality is no rose garden.

Another difficulty in trying to look ahead is even more fundamental. The actions resulting from a managerial decision, say with respect to a new process or product, may affect more than one group of people. And the effects may be quite different for different groups. The manager must, in the first instance, consider the economic welfare of his firm above the economic welfare of other firms. Competitors and those standing in a competitive relationship, to be sure, are beyond the legal reach of the manager and firm. He may not, by law, concern himself with their well being, except in limited ways. Suppliers and buyers, on the other hand, especially of a large firm, tend to fall into the zone of concern. But how to judge an action which benefits A, harms B, and is neutral to C, especially when law and convention permit the action and business judgment applauds it?

To be sure, questions of health, safety, social stability, and all the other nonbusiness effects of a firm's behavior take precedence, in a civilized society, over the effects of a firm's action on its income statement or balance sheet. But a firm or manager cannot in good conscience, I believe, fail to follow a policy *because* it might hurt a competitor, even put him out of business while helping the consumer.

This was the economic dilemma faced by the Carter administration and the Congress in the spring of 1978. Inflation had reached painful levels and showed no signs of abating. Farmers felt their incomes were too low. To raise farm supports would hurt consumers via the price effect. Not to raise farm supports would hurt farmers.

The dilemma is obvious. The way out might have been to think of different ways either to hold back the untoward forces or to help farmers, or both. Without suggesting a solution, one may assert that the imaginative consideration of long and short term policies eluded both administration and congressional minds. But one must remember that not all social problems are soluble to the benefit of all involved. The government through its taxing power can assist business to look ahead. Especially in a period of rising prices the capital problem of business is severe. Rising costs tend to force business to operate within a brief investment horizon. Current activity and flows become more important than future strength. But since the control of the future depends on current savings, investment, and research, a sharp focus mainly on the present is desirable for neither the firm nor the society. Retained earnings are swallowed up in depreciation and maintenance. New capital is hard to come by. The division of the national dividend between consumption and savings does not reflect the needs of the future. A more rational tax structure might alleviate this situation.

Thus far we have established the argument that *general* rules for an ethical structure are not easily constructed. We therefore seek a middle ground, one of partial generalizations for rules and structure.

Ethics not only justifies social behavior but by justifying constraints too limits action in certain forms of behavior. What is implied in this notion is that the actor, the doer, is one with power, but one who recognizes restraints (not necessarily legal). The manager may do something out of the routine and the expected, but not in violation of law and ideology. A person with power, in any society, is generally restricted in the full use of that power if the effects on others are drastic and beyond social acceptance. Parents cannot whomp their children beyond what law and convention allow, although school-teachers, the Supreme Court has ruled, can paddle kids, only with the restraint of a possible assault charge. Ethical restraints on behavior may go beyond conventions and law. A manager may fire those close to him, change product lines, close or open plants, or reorganize the firm's structure. Actions such as these are permissible if in his opinion they will enhance the position of the firm. He should not, however, favor a friend or family member or refuse to deal with particular ethnic groups, and engage in other such discriminatory actions, even if they are considered legally permissible. Above all the implications of his managerial behavior on those not directly affected by his actions should be on his mind. The manager looks outward.

Under normal circumstances of dynamic change—that is, in situations short of revolution, famine, fire or flood—most issues of ethical business conduct which cause concern are peripheral to ordinary market behavior.

Monopoly in business is a potential evil. This is part of the common law, and of folk wisdom. But where does monopoly begin and competition end? The guidelines on anti-trust of the Department of Justice, in their entirety, satisfy virtually no one who is interested in the complex issues involved. The guidelines are fairly mechanical rules of relative market share allowable under differing conditions of industrial structure. So many competitors of such and such a size are within the approved lines; if there are fewer competitors of larger size, the firms are subject to anti-trust action.[6] The danger of mechanical interpretation and administration is obvious.

But guidelines are needed. Monopoly, in the legal sense, may be defined as a large, effective agglomeration of economic power compared to those buying and selling in the same or closely related markets. But at what degree of concentration does the accumulation of market power pose a threat, and at what level is it a mere inconvenience? We are all faced with the marginal or peripheral, hypothetical question. For industry and banking, the marginal cases also become, realistically, serious questions. It would be contrary to any reasonable application of the doctrine of implication to react by demanding "Off with their monopoloid heads."[7]

The effects of the accumulation of business power through the acquisition by growth, merger, or purchase of enormous capital may, in fact, be associated with high levels of output and with low prices. Nor is it at all clear that the recurrent cycles in trade may not, to a degree, at least, be minimized or alleviated by high levels of agglomeration. It may also be argued that further development and growth, on a general, rational scale, rather than being discouraged may be hastened by the accumulations of power. Such results seem to be benefits to the social welfare.

Yet a society based on democracy, statute, and constitution, cannot tolerate great concentrations of economic power without developing the capacity to restrain them, if need be. Restraints are imposed on great concentrations of power not because of what has happened, or even is likely to happen, but because of *what might* happen. The fear is analogous to the care and concern businessmen and lawyers evidence in the preparation of important contracts. As many contingencies as possible are covered.

Business development does not, it seems, exactly parallel the development of other social institutions insofar as the power to act without regard to moral and ethical norms is concerned. Business, tending to be large and with a technical base, probably tends to be less influenced by normal, i.e., restrained social debate and pressure than is usually assumed. The requirements of technology and the sheer power and size of the large corporation may tend to make it less reactive to public opinion than would be the case were the corporation less insulated. Also business structure is different (not necessarily more or less complex) from other social institutions, so that blame or responsibility is hard to assess against a given person or action. But the clamor of an articulate, aroused group, which can win the attention of the Congress and the administration will be listened to and compromised with. The nuclear debate, and the oil-energy debate are examples of the shift of peripheral concerns to central issues.

Issues of market share, price fixing, or reciprocal buying are not likely to generate much public excitement. Antipollution measures become unacceptable if they are assumed to cause unemployment. Other examples might be given, but all may be encapsulated in the phrase that issues in business ethics, in general, are not very interesting to the general public. It might even be, and probably is the case, that a great many of the legal restrictions on business are not in accord with conceptions of ethical business behavior which many people hold. In many large firms, and small, the responsible manager or managers are unknown to the public and even to the shareholders. How many people can name offhand the president or chairman of ATT, of Exxon, of the Metropolitan Insurance Company, of Chase Manhattan? For smaller firms the responsible heads are even less well known. Such anonymity is a kind of protective shield. But responsibility cannot be evaded, legally or ethically.

The responsibility of managers is great, but so is their latitude. It is not infrequent for critics of some public spirited action of a large corporation to assert that management is misapplying the funds of the company. For example, Exxon, Hartford Insurance, DuPont and other companies sometimes subsidize purely "artistic" endeavors on public television, or provide funds for scholarships. There appears, from time to time, criticism that such activity does not add to the income of the companies, and so, in effect, diverts funds from the owners to some noble but irrelevant activity. A similar criticism is made when it is discovered that a company keeps a drunk on the payroll, or overlooks some small, improper act of an employee.

Such criticisms, we hold, are ill conceived and unwarranted as serious indictments. When a manager is appointed, he in truth becomes the surrogate of the owners. Their responsibility has been delivered to him. An expenditure on Shakespeare or schlock is, by indirection, their approved policy if the manager approves it. "Manager" is "owner" writ small but effectively. If the manager believes that a public spirited act, e.g., of beautifying the grounds or going beyond mandated antipollution requirements, is worthwhile, the owners have no legitimate gripe. The manager may be heading off adverse criticism, or he may have an eye for beauty, or an antipollution complex, but his decision is the owners', at least for the period of his employment. If the owners do not approve managerial behavior, the manager can be admonished, advised, fired; or the owners can divest themselves of their holdings. But the manager *qua* manager is not acting in an untoward manner. He may be incompetent and foolish, but he is within his rights.

A related question is the social effect of business decisions. A significant issue involved in this external aspect of business is the determination of the point at which a corporation sets standards which, in effect, make public policy. An example is the conduct of a trade association, such as that in the motion picture industry, in policing itself regarding pornography, or the auto industry in determining antipollution standards. There may be a major objection to industrial self-policing, so called, with respect to any behavior which has a social impact. Industry standards for fittings and parts, as an example, may well adversely affect some producers. But if the affected firms can easily comply, no issue arises. If the new standards are onerous, the issues are more complicated. The pre–World War 2 Hayes Code of Morals in the motion picture industry probably dampened the artistic and social quality of movies and so deprived moviegoers of entertainment. Information gathering and sharing by trade associations can easily be a step toward collusive activity. The courts have not looked with favor on self-policing, and with good cause. The pollution problems, on the net, have been badly handled by industry. The safe limit of the manager seems to be to conduct his firm in a responsible fashion, consonant with law, convention, and his ethical values, or to lobby the Congress for appropriate laws or changes in the laws. "Public service" advertising—that is, advertising to affect public opinion and conventions—may sometimes be beyond socially allowable limits in the United States.

The task of the manager with respect to owners may be summarized as:

1. To assure the highest level of profitability. But profitability is either a long or short run conception, and often an accounting artifact. Roughly, a rate of profit in line with the market is to be expected.

2. To assure the perpetuity of the investment, or value of the capital stock. A business is a sometime thing, but capital is perpetual. The manager's task is to keep it so.

3. To assure salability of the firm. This means, in brief, that the ongoing firm can be converted to cash via sale of securities, of assets, or of the product which can be capitalized into a salable entity.

These conditions, and in any specific instance there are others, define the essential task of the manager. The constraints on his behavior are in the goals set for him. The three business essentials—profits, perpetuity, and salability—are not clearly defined, nor can they be; nor are they independent of each other. One essential always implies the others. But as any businessman knows, profitability can be measured in a number of ways, and for different time spans. So with salability. A firm, its products, or its securities cannot be traded every day of the year with the same chance of success. Perpetuity of capital is really the nub of the manager's problem. If the firm grows and prospers, perpetuity is at least not being denied. If the firm declines, the situation is threatening. If the firm is static, it is in trouble, for the business world is dynamic, and to be static in a growth situation is in effect to decline.

But the realization of the three goals implies a fourth which is logically prior to them. The manager, as a prerequisite, must assure that the firm achieves social acceptability. Obviously laws must be obeyed. But in addition the firm must appear to its buyers as well as to others that it is acting within the vaguely defined limits of acceptable behavior. Henry Ford's attack on Jewry in the 1920s hurt the company. In more recent times automobile firms, breakfast food manufacturers, the television industry, "ethical" drug houses, to name a few businesses have been criticized in the news media and by government bodies as not acting "in the public interest." This implies that their social acceptability has been questioned. Public pressure is always present in such circumstances.

The arrangements between manager and owners are usually not explicitly stated. Indeed in a large corporation there may be a number of different signals which management receives from the several segments of ownership. But the manager is the responsible head of the business, and it is in his warrant to act in what he conceives to be the best interests of the firm.

With this background in mind, let us again look at the three levels of ethical behavior.

1. The Minimal Ethic. The reader will recall that, at this level, the relations we were looking at were between the firm and individual respondents—a buyer, a seller, an employee. Most of the problems are amenable to conventional solutions or the application of law. Many of the issues, perhaps most, are small. The ethical questions are typically those which have to do with *going beyond normal behavior*—showing generosity of spirit (and money). The bread of generosity cast on the waters may come back as eggs benedict, but this cannot be guaranteed. Generosity may be the better part of self-interest. Good will is hard to define but very useful when needed.

But these are not the essence of the Minimal Ethic. Policy should be flexible at this level. The essence is that, with the markedly unequal power of the firm as compared to an individual or entity of lesser power, goodness in the abstract may be served by allowing a little more than is required. How to delegate the right to do good, in the name of the firm, is a delicate matter, but each organization must allow some leeway in the decision making authority to delegated subordinate managers and administrators. The nature of generosity is that it does not become a precedent; it is a privilege growing out of power.

2. The Big Ethic. This belongs to the market. As in the Minimal Ethic, law and convention are assumed as constraints on behavior. When and how to go beyond law and convention, and what to do when law and convention are silent, are the issues. If, after adequate internal debate, the manager cannot decide on the ethical stand he should take, the resolution of the issue may be sought in legislation or by judicial review. Many such issues are trivial, and fall under the Minimal Ethic. But the multiplicity of laws and court decisions on particular issues makes it virtually impossible to speak coherently of American business policy. Some legal and judicial vagueness might be desirable to assure flexibility, but vagueness can be a threat too.

It is not unreasonable to argue that the United States has no coherent anti-trust policy. Bigness is at once suspect and warmly regarded. Market power is defined so as to make it an evil, or at least an invitation to evil. Yet it seems that market power often tends to be associated with high output at lower cost than might have prevailed with smaller units. Profits sometimes appear to be higher than the market rate, but is this a prelude to some desirable social end such as plant expansion? To restrict the *firm* to optimal size has a logical attraction. But in fact often "optimal" size *plants*— that is, ideally sized plants from a technical viewpoint—are often larger than required by competition. Optimality itself depends on the size of the market, just as the division of labor does.

At any rate, it is clear to anyone who has observed industry and markets over an extended period that American (and European) industry is made up of many heterogeneous units. Beyond the most basic principles which deny conspiracy (because it is secret and hence dangerous), uncontrolled monopoly or near monopoly (because of the difficulty of gaining social control over it once it is operating, or of divesting it), and other per se anathemas, a single set of rules to regulate industry is impossible to operate. Policy depends on what is wanted. Conflict within reasonable bounds may be viewed as effective social harmony. One would not expect the business world to go on without some conflict.

Our feeling is that the ideology of business regulation in America is neither very well defined nor clearly oriented. The big ethical issue of business is to attempt to bring the issues into focus in the Grand Ethic arena.

3. The Grand Ethic. This has to do with social policy arising from the relations among institutions. How business as an institution or complex of institutions feels about competition and autonomy and how it presents these views to government, consumer groups, or the press is of great importance. The ethical concern of business cannot be divorced from the hard facts of the market, production, pricing, employment, quality, and output. For industry to insist it will do its best is not enough. The laws and the conventions of our time require, and presuppose, interaction among all the major social institutions. For some industries or firms to have "understandings" with the Defense Department or for business to be deaf to the plaints

of consumers is to court trouble. The whole social system becomes dysfunctional when large segments of the society lose faith in the institutional framework. To hire retired generals as a payoff to the Defense Department or to throw parties to bribe government agencies and engage in other power plays is as short sighted a policy as a society can put together. New York City and the post-Watergate exposés have left deeper scars than many people realize.

The Grand Ethic arises from discussion, and from a willingness and capacity of all institutions to make the changes in accordance with the ideal of compromise. *Compromise is the ideal of a democracy.* If insistent demands of customers or government result in lower output than might otherwise be the case, then output will have to be at less than maximum. Society is not engaged in maximizing one variable, it seeks optimal (second best) solutions. There has been, in effect, a tradeoff, say, of health care for income, of education for capital accumulation, or what not. Goods are not the only Good. The ideals of economic theory or business efficiency are not necessarily the ideals of the society, and ethics has to do with the approach to ideals.

It is clear that a dynamic society never reaches a stable state. Stability is a figment of analysis, not a part of reality. Conflict, argument, disagreement, politics, are inherent in a dynamic society, and are ever present in an evolving or merely changing society. But ideally and realistically, evolution can, to a degree, be controlled by directing it within agreed upon constraints. Herein lies the secret of the Grand Ethic. If we are required to give a name to our relatively free, dynamic society, we should call it, with all its failings, the Fortunate Society of the Second Best.

NOTES

1: A STRUCTURE OF BUSINESS ETHICS

1. W. J. Baumol, "On the Proper Cost Tests for Natural Monopoly in a Multi-Product Industry," *American Economic Review,* Dec. 1977; J. Robinson, "What Are the Questions?" *Journal of Economic Literature,* Dec. 1977, p. 1330; P. Sraffa, "The Laws of Return under Competitive Conditions," *Economic Journal,* Dec. 1926.

2. M. Polanyi and H. Prosch, *Meaning* (University of Chicago Press, 1975), ch. 3, "Reconstruction."

3. P. L. Berger and T. Luckmann, *The Social Construction of Reality* (Doubleday Anchor, 1967), pp. 92–128.

4. F. Modigliani, "The Monetarist Controversy," *American Economic Review,* March 1977, pp. 14ff.

5. Polanyi and Prosch, op. cit., pp. 59ff.

6. F. Machlup, "Operationalism and Pure Theory in Economics," in S. R. Krupp, ed., *The Structure of Economic Science* (Prentice-Hall, 1966), pp. 53ff.

7. J. W. Coleman, "Can We Revitalize Our Cities?" *Challenge,* Nov.-Dec. 1977; D. P. Moynihan, "How to Politicize the Economics of Growth, and Why Not To," mimeo, White House Conference on Balanced Growth and Economic Development, Jan. 1978.

8. R. M. Cyert and J. G. March, *Behavioral Theory of the Firm* (Prentice-Hall, 1963), ch. 2, "Antecedents of the Behavioral Theory of the Firm."

9. C. Ayers, *The Theory of Economic Progress,* 2d ed. (Schocken, 1944), ch. 10, "The Meaning of Value."

10. Robinson, op. cit., p. 1330.

2: THE MANAGEMENT TRAP

1. G. Odiorne, *Management and the Activity Trap* (Harper & Row, 1974).
2. K. Arrow, *The Limits of Organization* (Norton, 1975).
3. H. H. Liebhafsky, *Government and Business* (Wiley, 1971), ch. 13, "Concepts of Workable Competition."
4. G. C. Bjork, *Private Enterprise and Public Interest* (Prentice-Hall, 1969), ch. 1, "The Nature of Capitalism."
5. Odiorne, op. cit.
6. P. T. Heyne, *Private Keepers of the Public Interest* (McGraw-Hill, 1968), "Forms of Self-Deception," pp. 56ff.
7. O. E. Williamson, *Markets and Hierarchies* (Free Press, 1975), ch. 4, "Understanding the Employment Relationship."

3: THE FALLACY OF THE RABBLE HYPOTHESIS

1. E. Mayo, *Social Problems of an Industrial Society* (Harvard, 1945), esp. ch. 1.
2. C. Walton, "Overview," in C. Walton, ed., *Ethics of Corporate Conduct* (Prentice-Hall, 1977); also ch. 7, "The Executive Ethic."
3. C. W. Churchman, *The Challenge to Reason* (McGraw-Hill, 1968), ch. 12, "Theoretical Management."
4. L. Silk and D. Vogel, *Ethics and Profits* (Simon and Schuster, 1977).
5. C. E. Lindblom, *Politics and Markets* (Basic Books, 1977), esp. pp. 152ff.
6. N. W. Chamberlain, *Enterprise and the Environment* (McGraw-Hill, 1968), pp. 143ff.

4. THE DEATH OF DIOGENES

1. S. Becker and D. Neuhauser, *The Efficient Organization* (Elsevier, 1975), ch. 3, "Complexity of Task-Environment," pp. 69ff.
2. K. E. Boulding, *The Organizational Revolution* (Chicago: Quadrangle, 1968), ch. 8, "Business Organizations," pp. 131ff.
3. F. H. Knight, *On the History and Method of Economics* (University of Chicago Press, 1956), ch. XII, "Free Society: Its Basic Nature and Problems."
4. P. Hersey and K. Blanchard, *Management of Organizational Behavior* (Prentice-Hall, 1977), 3rd ed., pp. 30ff.
5. J. E. Post, *Corporate Behavior and Social Change* (Reston, 1978), "When Public Values Change," pp. 107ff.
6. J. Monson, *Modern American Capitalism* (Houghton-Mifflin, 1963).

7.   A. Booth, "Introduction to Commentaries and Codes," in I. Hill, ed., *The Ethical Basis of Economic Freedom* (American Viewpoint, 1976), p. 257.
8.   N. Offen, "Direct Selling Association," in Ivan Hill, ed., op. cit., pp. 264ff.
9.   I. Hill, ed., *The Ethical Basis of Economic Freedom* (American Viewpoint, 1976).

5. ISN'T CITY HALL ON OUR TURF?

1.   L. B. Birdzell, "Business, Government, and the Walls Between," in N. H. Jacoby, ed., *The Business-Government Relationship* (Goodyear, 1975), pp. 20ff; J. W. Coleman, "Can We Revitalize Our Cities?" *Challenge* Nov.-Dec. 1977.
2.   R. G. Noll, "The Social Costs of Government Intervention," in N. H. Jacoby, ed., op. cit., pp. 56ff.
3.   G. F. Bloom and H. R. Northrup, *Economics of Labor Relations,* 7th ed. (Irwin, 1973), pp. 552ff.
4.   M. Green, "Toward Social Capitalism," in F. Luthans and R. M. Hodgetts, eds., *Social Issues in Business* (Macmillan, 1976), pp. 509ff.
5.   M. Ways, "A Plea for Perspective," in C. Walton, ed., *The Ethics of Corporate Conduct* (Prentice-Hall, 1977).

6: SHOULD I TELL MY PARTNER?

1.   F. H. Knight, *Freedom and Reform* (Harper, 1947), ch. 3, "Pragmatism and Social Action," and ch. 4, "Ethics and Economic Reform."
2.   J. Ortega y Gassett, *Concord and Liberty* (Norton, 1946), ch. 1, "Concord and Liberty."
3.   C. Madden, "Forces Which Influence Ethical Behavior," in C. Walton, ed., *Ethics of Corporate Conduct* (Prentice-Hall, 1977).
4.   G. C. Lodge, "Managerial Implications of Technological Change," in Walton, ed., op. cit.
5.   W. G. Shepherd and C. Wilcox, *Public Policies Toward Business,* 6th ed. (Irwin, 1979), ch. 10, "Tasks and Forms of Regulation."
6.   W. James, *The Philosophy of William James,* H. Kallen, ed. (Modern Library, 1925). See esp. "Philosophy and the Philosopher," pp. 59ff., and "The World We Live In," pp. 82ff.
7.   J. M. Clark, *Social Control of Business* (McGraw-Hill, 1939), ch. 3, "Business: Private Right or Public Interest?" and ch. 4, "Purposes of Social Control."
8.   J. S. Berliner, *The Innovative Decision in Soviet Industry* (MIT Press, 1976). See preface.

7: WHAT TO DO UNTO OTHERS?

1.   N. Cooper, "Morality and Importance," in G. Wallace and A. D. M. Walker, eds., *The Definition of Morality* (Methuen, 1970), pp. 91ff.

2. S. Hook, *The Hero in History* (Beacon Press, 1947), pp. 165ff.

3. T. V. Smith, *Philosophic Ways of Life in America*, 2d ed. (Kennikat Press, 1968), pp. 48ff.

4. T. C. Schelling, "Command and Control," in J. McKie, ed., *Social Responsibility and the Business Predicament* (Brookings, 1974), p. 80.

5. Smith, op. cit., pp. 82ff.

8: DOING THINGS RIGHT

1. P. Bridgman, *The Intelligent Individual and Society* (Macmillan, 1938), ch. 1, "The Intelligent Individual and Society"; ch. 2, "Suggestions from Physics," pp. 38–47; J. Dewey, *Human Nature and Conduct* (Modern Library, 1922), pp. 206–9.

2. C. E. Barnard, "The Theory of Authority," in Parsons, Shils, Negler, and Pitts, *Theories of Society* (Free Press, 1961), 1: 632ff.

3. S. C. Sufrin and S. Paul, *Small Sellers and Large Buyers in American Industry* (College of Business Administration, Syracuse University, 1961).

4. J. E. Post, *Corporate Behavior and Social Change* (Reston, 1978), ch. 1, "The Frontiers of Management," pp. 3ff.

5. Ibid., ch. 11, "Politics and Management," pp. 217–19.

6. F. M. Scherer, *Industrial Market Structure and Economic Performance* (Rand McNally, 1971), pp. 440ff.

7. J. K. Galbraith, *The New Industrial State* (Houghton Mifflin, 1967), pp. 184ff.; R. A. Solo, *Economic Organizations and Social Systems* (Bobbs-Merrill, 1967), ch. 16, "Decentralized Market Direction As a Social Environment"; ch. 17, "The Economy of Autonomous Organizations As a Social Environment."

INDEX